The Rockstars of JVZoo.com

The Rockstars of JVZoo.com

How Regular People Have Made a Fortune Buying and Selling on the World's Fastest-Growing Ecommerce Platform

JOEL COMM

New York

The Rockstars of JVZoo.com
How Regular People Have Made a Fortune Buying and Selling on the World's Fastest-Growing Ecommerce Platform

Published in New York, New York, by Morgan James Publishing. Morgan James and The Entrepreneurial Publisher are trademarks of Morgan James, LLC. www.MorganJamesPublishing.com

The Morgan James Speakers Group can bring authors to your live event. For more information or to book an event visit The Morgan James Speakers Group at www.TheMorganJamesSpeakersGroup.com.

A **free** eBook edition is available with the purchase of this print book.

CLEARLY PRINT YOUR NAME ABOVE IN UPPER CASE

Instructions to claim your free eBook edition:
1. Download the BitLit app for Android or iOS
2. Write your name in **UPPER CASE** on the line
3. Use the BitLit app to submit a photo
4. Download your eBook to any device

ISBN 978-1-63047-587-1 paperback
ISBN 978-1-63047-588-8 eBook
Library of Congress Control Number:
2015903040

Interior Design by:
Bonnie Bushman
bonnie@caboodlegraphics.com

In an effort to support local communities and raise awareness and funds, Morgan James Publishing donates a percentage of all book sales for the life of each book to Habitat for Humanity Peninsula and Greater Williamsburg.

Get involved today, visit
www.MorganJamesBuilds.com

Habitat
for Humanity®
Peninsula and
Greater Williamsburg
Building Partner

Table of Contents

Preface

Rockstars of JV Zoo
Preface by Joel Comm
New York Times Best-Selling Author of 11 Books

When it comes to the online business world, it truly is a jungle out there. So many people are competing for Internet attention and looking for ways to generate revenue.

One of the best ways for regular people to make money online from home through the creation and sales of information products. These how-to manuals, videos software tools and membership sites help consumers find the solutions they are looking in a way that is instantly gratifying. Simply purchase the product and receive access without having to go to the store or wait for a product to arrive in the mail.

Not only are thousands of people discovering their ability to share their expertise through their own products, but countless more are presenting these products and services to their website visitors, email subscribers and social media following as affiliates. That is, by simply sharing a product or service with a specially coded link, these savvy entrepreneurs are generating commissions from each and every sale.

I've been doing this for almost two decades, and have earned some handsome commissions along the way.

But as the Internet has evolved, so have the tools which facilitate doing business. I've seen a number of networks which connect merchants to affiliates over the years, but one network has really grabbed my attention.

That network is JVZoo.com.

I first became aware of JVZoo.com shortly after they launched their site just a few years back. They had developed a simple, yet sophisticated method of connecting information product creators with a large network of affiliates eager to promote and present their products to their own audience.

In under three years, JVZoo.com had processed over $100,000,000 in transactions, and that number is increasing daily.

As I spoke with the creator of JVZoo.com, E. Brian Rose, I suggested to him that amongst his top merchants and affiliates, there existed some great success stories which would inspire others seeking to build a full or part-time business online.

This book is the fruit of that idea. Within these pages, you will discover the stories of regular people who have either created their own information products, or become super affiliates generating commissions from promoting other peoples' products, through the JVZoo.com system.

I think you'll be inspired and encouraged to explore the opportunities that exist for anyone to take control of their financial future by discovering how to make money on the Internet.

It's not only a jungle out there, but apparently, it's also a zoo. A JV Zoo. Enjoy.

Foreword

Listen. Do you hear it? It's that voice inside of you that wants something different. Something better. More time with the family. More money in your bank account. A future that is determined by you. We all have that inner voice. Isn't it time you listened to yours?

There has never been a more perfect time to start thinking about entrepreneurship. Pension plans and gold watches are a thing of the past. To be successful in today's world, you need to think outside of the box. The days of working for the same company for your entire career and retiring are gone.

Just three years ago, the unemployment rate was hovering around ten percent. Jobs were few and far between, and people, young and old, were wondering what their futures was going to look like. That is when I co-founded a company called JVZoo.com. It gave people the opportunity to create their own jobs, without relying on others.

JVZoo is an online marketplace where we match up creators of digital products with affiliates that who will promote those products for a commission. Within days of the site's launch, ordinary people were uploading everything from e-books to instructional videos to software. Anyone with a FaceBook account or a blog was a potential affiliate.

It's really quite simple. Joe adds an e-book about how to lose weight after the holidays. Suzy sees this e-book in the marketplace and thinks her FaceBook friends might be interested. She grabs her affiliate link and includes it in a post. When her friends buy the e-book, Suzy makes money.

Or maybe you're are more the creative type. We all have experience in something. Sharing your knowledge can be very lucrative. It doesn't matter what the topic is, people are willing to pay for things that make their life lives easier. Did you figure out a way to pay off your credit cards early? Write a short report about it, and just like that, you are an e-book author.

Rockstars of JVZoo is a compilation of case studies, written by people, just like you, that people who listened to their inner voices and created a jobs for themselves. Everything you are about to read has been achieved by ordinary people who did that one thing that separates entrepreneurs from the rest of society: they took action.

In the three years that JVZoo has been around, its members have generated over $100 million in sales revenue. Our members are mainly made up of people that who started making money online as a part- time venture.

JVZoo is an amazing resource for entrepreneurs to turn their knowledge into digital products and recruit hundreds or thousands in their field to promote those products. Whether you are a business consultant, lawyer, real estate agent, or even someone that who knows how to build the perfect birdhouse, JVZoo allows you to put your knowledge into a format that can be sold and profited from. While the rest of the world looks for jobs, our members create their own.

It's time you start listening to your inner voice. Read these stories and take action. Nobody will determine your future, except for you.

Sincerely,

E. Brian Rose

Persuade Yourself
To Live Your Dreams

by Scott Smith

How is it possible I can be thundering down the highway, riding my Harley, thinking about how…someday…I will actually start doing what I was meant to in this life? My purpose in life must be greater than spitting bugs out of my teeth on a hot Florida day, after all.

Do you know your purpose? I'm fond of teaching that "if you don't know your purpose in life, your purpose is to find your purpose." You might just get lucky and stumble onto what you really love, which is in direct conflict with modern self-help teachings. Still, I believe that most folks are at least a little bit happy with their lives, even if they won't admit it. Why would you get out of bed every morning to do what you do if it didn't work for you in some small way?

I like to talk about these things because my podcast listeners like to hear about these things. They call it ScottLOGIC and they've been eating it up since 2006 when I started podcasting. I have since become know by some people as the "Podcast King." To date, I've hosted and produced over 7,124 podcasts and created the most-downloaded daily motivation and self-help podcast in the history of iTunes, called <u>The Daily Boost</u>. And my mom thought I would never amount to anything!

Speaking of Mom…Recently, I visited her at her home in the beautiful Shenandoah Valley of Virginia. We were having a catch-up conversation, and she said she was very proud of me—something we never get too old to hear. My journey from outspoken teenager, to FM radio "shock jock," to finally helping millions of people improve their lives wasn't something you would have found written on the back page of my high school yearbook.

Like most folks, I spent my life chasing dreams, until the day I stumbled upon podcasting and never looked back. I would never have expected my happiness to come in the form of an MP3 file, distributed in bits and bytes all over the world so that eventually Mom could listen to me on her iPhone at two times normal speed.

Podcasting literally gave my voice. After 7,124 episodes, my mom had one simple question: "How did you manage to pick yourself up and keep going through all those episodes?"

She was referring to Labor Day weekend in 2006. By coincidence, I had decided to start my first business based on podcasting on the same day I was moving out of my recently-sold home. As if that weren't enough, it was the very same day my first wife received a terminal cancer diagnosis that would rock our world and see us crossing into an entirely new threshold of our lives. But I knew everything would be okay when my wife said to me, "It's a bummer, for sure, but don't you have a podcast to record?"

I simply said, "Yes, honey," and walked off to my studio.

Together we had both embarked upon a journey of motivating and helping others, and my podcast was our first success. Always positive, Sheryl made me promise to continue to share our story while she was ill and after she was gone. I haven't stopped yet.

I've often wondered how other folks experience life's hard times and end up making life better. If you're asking the same question about my story, all I can say is, that's just the way it works.

Honestly, if Mom had asked me that question in the heat the moment, when we were dealing with life and death, I wouldn't have had an answer that made any sense at all. I was just living and doing, caught up in the millisecond that is "the moment," with no worry of the moment before or after. But now, more seasoned and sitting on the other side of the 10,000 hour rule, it seems to all come down to two words: persistence and persuasion.

I've always been good at being stubborn; persistence is just a fancy word for that. Just ask my mom. I figure that if I keep showing up, eventually things will go my way. Getting yourself to show up so you <u>can</u> be persistent requires a healthy dose of self-persuasion, but your success will always come from your ability to persuade yourself to be persistent long enough to get what you want.

So now we're down to only persuasion. Our journey begins when we decide there is something we would like to do with our lives, and we promise ourselves that we'll do it this time. In that moment we revert to childhood, learning for the first time that we don't always have to do what our parents ask—and that we might get away with it.

Now, as full-grown, tax-paying, my-way-or-the-highway adults, we build on that initial experience when we realize that we don't actually have to do what <u>we</u> ask ourselves to, either. Have you ever had the following conversation with yourself?

"I'm the boss of me. I know what I said I was going to do, but I don't have to do what I said I was going to do. And you can't make me!"

Huh?

All successful and happy people on this planet are in a constant battle to persuade themselves to actually do what it takes to accomplish their dreams. Even if we want it more than anything else in the world, we still need to talk ourselves into it <u>every day</u>. This inner battle must be won if you ever hope to be content and happy with your life, but it is well worth the fight.

We must also persuade others. Think of it this way: Persuading yourself to accomplish a goal is the equivalent of revving your Harley's engine and banking your way through North Carolina's notorious Tail of the Dragon mountain. In other words, persuading others is like talking all of your best buddies into spending the weekend riding with you!

But how can it be that everything I've learned in over 7,124 podcast episodes comes down to persuading or being persuaded? Let's go back to that "purpose" thing for a moment.

My most popular podcast is called <u>The Daily Boost</u>—it's the positive boost you need every day. At only nine minutes in length, <u>The Daily Boost</u> is filled with

24-karat gold nuggets of wisdom designed to persuade you to live on purpose, design your own agenda, follow your dreams, and give you the tools to do so.

Besides the average folks who listen to me, I've had the pleasure to helping hundreds of people understand how to use the power of podcast persuasion to change lives and make a great living doing what they love. It's been an honor to hear their many voices affect so many other folks all over the world. But I have to tell you, in all the interactions with regular folks and podcasters over the years, I've learned that the lucky ones are those who successfully persuade themselves and others to live the life of their dreams.

How do you master persuasion even if you haven't done 7,124 podcasts? Persuading yourself begins with understanding that goal-setting is the heartbeat of your life. No lecture here. Not setting goals instantly puts you under the control of others. You don't even need to know <u>how</u> you will accomplish your goals, only <u>why</u> you will accomplish them. A strong enough why is all the persuasion you need to get the job done.

Since pursuing goals is essentially what you do to fill your days, this will automatically create your personal agenda, and that will create the experience you call life. Knowing your agenda will keep you from getting caught up in the agenda of others. More importantly, when you learn to persuade others to help <u>you</u> accomplish your goals, you accelerate and amplify yourself beyond your wildest dreams.

Could it be that simple? I think my mom would be proud of that answer, especially since she's the one who taught me the lesson to begin with.

About The Author

Known as the "Podcast King," Scott Smith is the founder and Chief Motivating Officer of <u>MotivationToMove.com</u>. He was one of the first to enter the world of podcasting in 2006 with the creation of <u>The Daily Boost</u> podcast—the most popular self-help podcast in the world and the most-downloaded self-help podcast in the history of iTunes with over 10 million downloads.

Scott was also one of the first to monetize a podcast utilizing a membership model and currently produces 16 podcasts per week for his members in 115 counties. To date, he has produced an incredible 7,124 podcast episodes, while optimizing his business to maintain a retention rate of 95 percent.

Today, Scott is the go-to expert for building and sustaining a #1 podcast and membership site, for monetizing and retention, as well as high-end coaching, consulting, and international speaking and business services.

You can connect with Scott at:

Facebook: http://facebook.com/scottsmithmtm

Twitter: @motivationtomove

To find out more about how Scott creates so many podcasts each week and how you can do it too, go to podcastpersuasion.com

Give Before Getting and Joint Venture Partnerships Done Right

by Brian G. Johnson

In 2008, I made a decision that changed my life in ways I could never have imagined. I decided to enter the Internet marketing space with the goal of sharing my Internet marketing ideas, strategies, and tactics that allowed me to escape my day job in 2003.

Two years later I earned $452,000 in profit—not gross revenue, mind you, but profit. I share this not to brag, but rather to highlight the fact that what I'm about to reveal is based on personal experience. I could not have achieved this level of success without partnering and working strategically with others. I'll discuss how to super charge your results by partnering with others and giving before getting.

First things first, know this: the success you desire is not hard to achieve. It's not hard at all, in fact. You don't need to be the smartest person in the room, you don't have to have a technical degree, a PhD, a fancy-pants license, or be a New York Times best-selling author. Of course, these accolades are great. But they're not necessary to achieve incredible financial results. I certainly didn't have any of these things.

Furthermore, what I'm about to share can be used by anyone regardless of race, religion, creed, or experience (or lack thereof) to absolutely crush it online. Millions and millions of incredibly successful, wealthy online entrepreneurs have not yet arrived. They are, however, staking their claim and forging a path to greatness. I invite you to decide right now that you're one of those undiscovered rock stars. I did it, Joel Comm did it, and so have many of my coaching students.

Now it's your turn, and in the coming pages I'll share with you the exact steps I took to develop powerful, strategic partnerships. It's financial success, in a nutshell.

• • • • •

In my humble opinion, the most important elements of success are believing it's possible, having clarity in how you'll deliver assets, and taking focused, daily actions to publish those assets.

• • • • •

That's it. Do that, and you'll be a massive success.

In 2008, I launched a blog that led to releasing my first product to the market. The focus of both was leveraging expired domains in a unique way that made it fairly easy to make money.

How I launched that first product led to sales, future joint venture partners, a highly responsive list, engagement with those in my community, and more. All the ingredients that lead to success. Mind you, I did this starting from ground zero, and you can, too.

Looking back, it was clear that I focused on two fundamentals that I live by today: to figure out what people want (and then to give it to them), and giving before getting. They're pretty simple concepts that may sound easy to do, but they're not so easy, and frankly, most do not do them.

Food for thought: marketing is about connecting with and working with people in numerous ways. You'll be asking people to sign up, share, buy, and review what you publish—whether it's a blog post, a Facebook status update, a software product, or a Kindle e-book.

You'll also be connecting and working with colleagues and partners. You'll support their efforts, and in return they'll support yours. Know this: it's much more difficult to achieve high-level success without the support of other successful entrepreneurs. That means you'll want to ask for their help. How you ask will make or break a potential lucrative partnership.

Partners who will share your product with their tribe can literally change your life overnight, but actually getting successful marketers to support your efforts takes planning, finesse, and outside-the-box thinking.

Many marketers get this wrong. They see the prize, they move forward in desperation or without really thinking through their actions, and they make a total mess of things. Here's why. Those who are brand new have not proven themselves, they have not yet developed a trusted personal brand, and they can't reciprocate with the same impact as someone who already has an established business online. Furthermore, highly successful marketers already work with others they know, like, and trust. They find partners who have the ability to drive substantial business back their way when it's their turn.

Why should they support you? Why should they take a risk on someone who has not yet proven himself? It's imperative that you give potential partners a good reason why, before asking for anything. When you're just starting out, don't make the rookie mistake of asking someone you have yet to build rapport with to support you. Instead, do something that addresses their needs and wants first. Give before getting.

These are the steps I took to do just that. Earlier I mentioned I started a blog prior to the launch of my first product. I had come up with a unique strategy for expired domains and I simply started sharing that strategy. That is, I was giving before getting.

I wasn't selling, nor setting up a prelaunch, but rather focusing on the needs and wants of those around me. First, I freely gave my ideas and tactics. Then, I offered a way for those interested to access more information either by signing up to a list or buying my product.

After a few months the blog had established a following. It was not a huge number of people but a core group of highly interested folks. I gave them what they wanted and they returned for more 'Brian G' strategies again and again.

Around this time I released a three-part series called Revenue Domains. The first post in the series was a hit, and people commented, engaged, and left their excitement for the next installment.

During this time, I thought that this topic would make for a great info product, and I asked my readers if they would be interested. They responded positively, so I took what I shared in the blog series, expanded it, and launched it as a product.

On Day 1 of my launch, many of my readers purchased, and I was well on my way. I had launched a blog that was driving traffic and building a list, and I had created videos on the same topic, which were also driving traffic via YouTube. I had begun to build my personal brand and was establishing trust with my audience. I had done this with no joint venture partners, no ad budget, no elaborate marketing strategy. Rather, I simply focused on the needs and wants of others to kick-start my brand.

This was my springboard. I had a product, buyers, a list, and assets that I could strategically leverage, and that's exactly what I did. I then asked myself, "What is it that my subscribers want, and do I know any marketers who could fill that need?"

I did not focus on getting hundreds of partners onboard for my next launch, but rather focused on establishing relationships with other marketers I trusted. Then I approached them about setting up a promotion for their product. That is, I would promote their product to my list of subscribers and buyers.

Of course, nearly all the potential partners I approached loved the idea. Instead of the usual "Will you promote my product?" pitch, I asked to promote theirs. Give before getting.

The results?

I provided my subscribers with products I believed in and that were well-suited to their needs. Thus, my subscribers won, and in the process I was able to generate sizable affiliate commissions and most of the partners asked what type of products I had available.

Bingo.

After launching my third product, Commission Ritual, I remember thinking that an easy-to-use keyword research tool would be well-received by my buyers and subscribers. I contacted James Jones, a high level marketer with a sizable list and the creator of a great keyword research tool. I asked to have a webinar with him to demo his software and its usage to my audience.

This resulted in awesome earnings for both James and me, and during that webinar, James asked what kinds of products I had. In the next 30 days, James and I ran two webinars for my product. Ka BOOM!

Find what people want and give it to them, and give before getting. These simple strategies can take you very far in your business.

Before I leave you, understand that some potential partners may make a mess of things themselves. You'll send them business, leads, and money, and they may not reciprocate. If you continue on this path and give, however, you'll find that you're rewarded in other ways, sometimes by people who contact YOU to support your product.

Expect bumps in the road, but enjoy the journey. Because that's what life and business are really all about. The everyday journey.

Best,

Brian G. Johnson

People do not fail at Internet marketing, they simply give up before the magic happens.

About the Author

Brian G. Johnson is a serial entrepreneur who is also an engaging speaker, product creator, #1 best-selling author, nurturing mentor, and passionate poodle wrangler. Since 2008, Brian has coached tens of thousands of wealth seekers, many of whom are successfully generating life-changing income.

Brian's high energy and zest for life translate well into his coaching programs, where he breaks down the most important elements characteristic to many profitable online businesses—traffic and conversions. His formulas are simple, his rituals are effective, and his techniques are rather easy to follow.

Learn more about Brian and his powerful Internet marketing strategies at:

MarketingEasyStreet.com

Facebook: facebook.com/marketingeasystreet

YouTube: YouTube.com/user/marketingeasyst

Google+: plus.google.com/u/0/+BrianGJohnson-MarketingEasySt
Twitter: @marketingeasystreet

Rockstar Entrepreneur Manifesto: For Those of Us Who Believe in Doing Less For More

by Ben Littlefield

'm sure you immediately jumped to this section of this book to hear my story—the story about a boy who grew up to sling digital "crack" online to support his family and buy lots of stuff. Maybe you want to see pictures of cool cars, blingy jewelry, and screenshots of the latest earnings? I know. This is what I always look for when I am seeking sage advice and knowledge.

If this is the case, I have bad news. I regret to inform you that I am going to bypass this obnoxiousness altogether. The good news, however, is that you probably don't care about what I can brag about anyway. Instead, I hope you'll find it useful for me to share how you can actually be a little bit lazy and still get much more wealthy, the way I have for the past six years. Let's talk about what it is to be a "Rockstar Entrepreneur."

What is a Rockstar Entrepreneur? First, it is my full belief that entrepreneurs make the world go round. They are the innovators who bring solutions to problems. They are the ones who put others to work. They are, in their own right, rock stars. The evolution of entrepreneurship is interesting and has evolved over time.

To better understand, let's look at a brief (and recent) history of entrepreneurship. First came Think and Grow Rich by Napoleon Hill, which illustrated how successful entrepreneurs looked at the world differently. This led to a generation of entrepreneurs who embraced abundant thinking. Then came the era of Zig Ziglar, who taught us that if we are not successful, it is our own fault. This led to a revolution of entrepreneurs, non-victims who owned their fate. Then we were blessed with The E-Myth by Michael E. Gerber, which spawned the process-oriented entrepreneur. Flash forward to The 4-Hour Work Week by Tim Ferriss, which showed us how we can better leverage our time. Throughout this process we have evolved to a new age of entrepreneurial thought.

Where does the evolution of entrepreneurial thought bring us? Simple. With the advent of online connectivity and the ease of access to information, resources, and transaction, we are living in an era in which we can, in fact, stop allowing our businesses to own us. We are in the middle of a very special movement, a revolution that allows us to do what we love rather than hate what we do.

The sad truth is, there are lots of folks who feel completely trapped. They either work in a job they dislike or have to miss out on time with their family, kids, or friends. These people sacrifice more and more every day. The dreaded commute can be enough to drive them crazy. Perhaps the thought that strangers are raising their kids leaves them feeling uncomfortable in the life they lead. Or maybe they just hate the loud, obnoxious dude in the next cubicle who talks about all the women he wants to date. And don't get me started on those crazy coworkers who are always complaining about their personal drama!

All of these things above are mentioned without judgment. No one wants to feel like they have no control over the life they are living. No six-year-old says, "I want to be miserable and powerless when I grow up." I realize I am preaching to the choir when I say this.

Do you know my number one fear in life? It is a fear of not spending time with my family. I have nightmares about not being able to be a part of my kids' lives. It terrifies me to think about sitting in traffic for two hours every day to go to a place I don't like, just to be a cog in a wheel. I panic when the idea enters my head.

It isn't because I don't value hard work. It is not because I lack respect for those who do it. It is simply because I have lived a different way. I have managed to construct my life the way I want it. It is no accident that I get up with my kids every morning. It isn't some stroke of luck that I get to spend several hours with my wife every evening, after we've read books to my boys and tucked them into their beds. It is, in fact, by design that I am home all weekend and am around for my family. It is even by design that I get to travel and enjoy the things I love with the people I love.

Is it easy to run a business? Isn't an Internet marketing business easy? No, and hell no. There is no such thing as <u>easy</u>. Truth is, it is all hard. But you must pick your poison. I'd love to tell you that building a multimillion dollar business is as simple as clicking a couple buttons and going about your day. It would be awesome to tell you that the life I am so proud to live is always easy. (Here you are, wishing I had just shown you those pictures of flashy cars and bling bling.)

The fact is, being an entrepreneur is hard. For me, it isn't because it requires work. No way. I don't consider what I do work, not even for a minute. Nope. The hard part is getting up when taking one on the chin.

Have you ever been excited about some genius idea that popped into your mind in the shower? This brilliant idea that would change the world and put you in the ranks of the elite? And have you told this idea to your closest confidant, who immediately told you every reason it would fail? Have you ever been that Debbie Downer who told someone his dreams sucked? Come on, we have all seen it, from both ends. This, my friend, is the hard part of the world of innovation.

The sheer will of ignoring the negative noise and silencing the doubt requires more strength than most are willing to burden. It takes serious confidence to do what we do. When failure becomes a fear that controls us, we surrender to the idea of "good enough." I call BS! If you are trapped by this thinking, I want you to change it and understand that the only failure is accepting "good enough." Acceptance of mediocrity is failure.

On the contrary, aiming for what you want is never failure. There are only two outcomes to going for the win:

1. Aim, fire, hit.
2. Aim, fire, miss, aim again, repeat.

It's us versus them. The choices are simple. You can let others dictate what you want, how you live, how you spend your time, and how you count down to the end of your life. Or you can choose to join the movement of Rockstar Entrepreneurs.

Traditional thought is that money is the motivation to own a business. That's not the case for this new breed. Money is great. Money is awesome. But money simply paves the way for the true prize that Rockstar Entrepreneurs aim for. Have you guessed it yet?

The prize is time. Time is everything. Money is money, money is easy. Money isn't even real. Money is some idea of a value printed on special paper. If I burn through $20,000—well, that would suck, but I could always make it back. Again, it was just some paper that was printed.

My time, however, is irretrievable. When my eldest son, Ted, graduates high school, that's it. I can't get the years back. There is no time machine that would give me the chance to read him a story every night and to be around to create memories for him. There is no chance my youngest boy, Axel, will learn to ride a bike twice. And I will be damned if I am not there. Time is the measure of wealth for a Rockstar Entrepreneur. Money is just the means to that end.

Here are the three crucial pillars to mastering the art of working less and making more:

1. Leverage.

This word certainly does get thrown around a lot. What is leverage to you? What does it mean in terms of achieving further freedom to gain "time wealth?" To put it in simple terms, I want you to envision your business and what it is you offer, how you sell it, how you service it, and how you get paid. Most would look at it as follows: you create an offer (which could be as simple as a service), and you sell it by doing the typical prospecting activities (networking, cold calling, et cetera). Then you deliver it by doing the work promised. That is how you get paid.

Do you see the flaw? This is still a job. This is not much different from punching a time clock. Owning a business like this may make you an entrepreneur, but owning a job certainly does not make you any better off. A Rockstar Entrepreneur leverages his or her time. What if, instead of offering a service to a client, you manipulated your skill set into delivering the results your client wants to achieve?

For a time I ran a marketing consulting business. In this business, I took on clients who paid me for website design, search engine optimization, and similar services. I actually made a lot of money. I also had a lot of bosses. I recall, at one point, having close to 100 of them. They called me at all hours, on weekends and holidays, and any time they pleased. I had a high-paying job that I owned, but zero time! That was, until I changed it.

How did I change it? Simple. Once I realized that the result my clients wanted was to get more leads for their respective organizations, it became very clear. I reduced my client load down to just one. You heard me right. Just one client! Me.

If all my clients really want at the end of the day is leads, I know how to do that. I have been doing that for them and know exactly how to do it. As my only client, I can get the results and sell those. In other words, now I own assets, rather than work for customers. My assets produce leads.

An example could be a website optimized for dentists in Houston. That is an asset I own and control, and it produces a result that generates income. It is mine, and I am no longer at the employ of a client. Now I am holding the key. I am the landlord. I am free.

This is leverage. It can be applied to just about any situation in business. It is the crucial piece to creating the lifestyle you want to create.

Instead of looking at your business as a function of what you offer, look at your business as an investment portfolio. You are now creating assets that you own and control that are capable of generating cash flow. This simple shift in thinking is huge. How can you turn your business into a set of cash-producing assets, as opposed to a singular offering that requires you to trade your time for money? Stop trading time and start leveraging it.

2. Awareness

Leverage is only going to take you so far. Awareness is likened to enlightenment in the eyes of a Rockstar Entrepreneur. Let me ask you, what business is Apple in? What business is Amazon in? Did you guess that Apple was in the computer and "smart gadget" business? Did you guess that Amazon was in the e-commerce business? If you did, you aren't entirely right. In fact, you are dead wrong.

Both Apple and Amazon are in the content distribution business. Simple as that. Sure, Apple releases cool gizmos and fancy computers. But did you know that their huge revenue generators are iTunes, iBooks, and the App Store? Sure you did, but now that it is more obvious, think about all those doodads they make. They are vehicles of distribution. An iPhone is not a smart phone. It is the ultimate content consumption machine, built to make it simple for you to buy songs, books, apps, you name it.

An Amazon Kindle or Amazon Fire tablet is the same. It is a gadget that makes it really easy for you to use the e-commerce engine of Amazon to consume the content, which is the point of it all.

Now that we have an awareness, can you be honest about what business you are truly in? Identifying this makes the whole leverage part much easier. If you understand, on an esoteric level, where your business fits in the universe it serves, innovation becomes automatic. Without it, no amount of leverage can ever save you from being obsolete.

3. Destination

This is a hard one for entrepreneurs: to know your destination. Why is it so hard? Because, if you're like me, you have ADHD, or as I prefer to call it: "ADHHHHHHHHHHHHHHHHHHHHHHHHHHHHD! Where was I? I just saw a squirrel."

Imagine someone blindfolds you, flies you to a random place, and removes your blindfold in front of a car. Then this person instructs you to drive the car. Your first question may be, "Where?" Good question. Now let's say they tell you to drive to Miami, Florida. Cool. Now you might want to know, "Where am I right now?"

This is all very logical. You probably wouldn't take a trip without having an idea of your destination. You certainly would be lost and unable to read any map, without knowing where you are. Why do we, as entrepreneurs, ignore this?

Have you ever just felt like every day might as well be the first day of your business? Has it ever felt like the movie Groundhog Day? You are just doing a bunch of stuff to get paid. By setting your destination and measuring that from your current location, it becomes easy to beat all the distracting noise that exists in the entrepreneurial mind.

In business, whether it is online, offline, outer space, or wherever, you will always drive to the destination. In other words, it is your ship to steer. Take control and enjoy the ride!

The Path of the Rockstar Entrepreneur

There is so much to gain and life is too short not to live it your way. Go live it. Build your business and grow your business to support the life you want and the time you want. It really is a matter of choice. If the path takes you toward that of a Rockstar Entrepreneur, awesome! In fact, join us. We have a whole free and supportive community of like-minded innovators who are changing the world. Come hang with us, read the blog, and listen to the podcast. You can find me and your fellow Rockstar Entrepreneurs at www. RockstarEntrepreneur.com

Rock On!

About the Author

Ben Littlefield is a RockStar serial entrepreneur. From running businesses since the age of 16 to teaching entrepreneurship at the University of Texas, his true mission is to change the world one RockStar Entrepreneur at a time.

Ben is a proud family man, a board member of JVZoo, and founder of a multimillion dollar digital media publishing, training, and consulting firm. For years, he has helped other entrepreneurs build businesses that provide true freedom. Many of his students have built businesses that have allowed them to work less and play more!

Connect with Ben at:

RockstarEntrepreneur.com

Facebook: facebook.com/BenLittlefield

Interviewing Lady Luck

by Michael Krisa

'm writing this chapter on the day it's due to Joel Comm, as the clock ticks down the time to the deadline and perspiration beads on my forehead. You might be thinking that 1) I procrastinate, and 2) I'm not good with deadlines, but nothing could be further from the truth.

What if I were to tell you that years ago I had one of the first syndicated podcasts for Realtors®? In fact, I did over 300 interviews with all the major CEOs, coaches, trainers, authors, and thought leaders in the real estate industry!

I had no formal training, no real qualifications to speak of, and no certifications. What I did have, and still do, however, is a genuine curiosity and interest in people.

It was my playground—getting people comfortable quickly and gently leading them in the right direction to get the kind of answers and content I knew my audience wanted.

What makes this story even more interesting is that it all started as a result of a random email I received one fine winter morning. It wasn't any ordinary email, no sir—it was an audio postcard, which at the time was like black magic!

The email was from Alex Mandossian, promoting an upcoming event. What was really intriguing to me was that the pitch was hidden within some really great audio content. It was a winning combination of message plus medium that kept me engaged for the entire ten minutes of audio. Keep in mind, this was 2003, when the Internet was still the Wild West and we relied on dial-up modems for connectivity. Clicking a button in an email and hearing a human voice from my speakers was friggin' amazing!

I had no idea how it was done or how I could do the same thing, but I knew I wanted to be able to do it. It opened up a world of possibilities. After weeks of Google searches and inquires, I finally received an email reply from Alex.

"It is Audio Generator," he said, "and it will be available soon. But here's a VIP link so you can get it now."

I was hooked, and $29 per month later, the ground work was laid for who I was to become and how I was to be branded. The Interview Guy® was born.

Next I needed someone to interview, someone big, someone everyone in real estate knew, who would create an instant draw. Enter David Lininger, founder of RE/MAX. He is bigger and bolder than life itself!

After much persuasion and pursuit, he finally agreed to a phone interview. I remember the evening we did the call. The phone rang, he answered, and my heart was racing. In the back of my mind I was thinking, "What if this is a bomb, what if I ask the wrong questions, what if I forget what to say…or even worse, what if there is no rapport?!"

For that fleeting moment, I was the proud owner of a luxury suite in Panic-ville, population 1. I was dog paddling in a pool of my own sweat.

Fortunately I am pretty quick-witted and remembered something a friend had shared with me. It was a little mind game to handle situations just like this, or when you have to make a major decision. You ask yourself, "What's the worst thing that can possibly happen?"

Well, survey says…death is the worst possible outcome of any situation, so if I don't die from this then it really isn't all that bad. LOL! After that it was a breeze. We did the interview, which took on a life of its own after a few minutes. Before I knew it, 70 minutes had passed!

Later that week, I had a website designed, added the audio button (thank you, Audio Generator), and sent it off to David for his approval.

My promise then, as it is to this day, is that my guest gets to hear or view a finished piece before it goes live. At that point they have three choices: 1) approve it and it goes live, 2) ask to do it over, or 3) reject the first two options and we walk away as friends, no harm, no foul. I am proud to say that after more than 300 interviews, option #3 has never been chosen.

David approved the audio interview, and we ran it. This is when it got really exciting. A few weeks later he called me out of the blue, asking if it would be okay to send the interview to all of his RE/MAX affiliates—at the time over 100,000 real estate professionals.

So what did I say? ABSO-FRIGGIN-LUTELY! But it had to be shared from the link on my website, which had the audio embedded within the page, and which also happened to have an opt-in box in the top right-hand corner.

David agreed, and within two weeks our subscriber list grew by 21,347!

Well, as they say in the shampoo business, wash, rinse, repeat. That's exactly what I did with every CEO of every major real estate franchise.

From there it was all the major coaches, trainers, and authors in the real estate space, and I was having a blast! They started calling me to be interviewed, and That Interview Guy® became a recognized brand.

Like any great ride, it doesn't take long before things start to get old—not necessarily for the passenger but for the guy behind the wheel (or in my case, behind the microphone). Don't get me wrong, I absolutely loved interviewing new guests, getting to know them, and sharing their strategies and stories, but after awhile it all started sounding the same to me. I needed something new but wasn't quite sure what that was yet.

Enter Mike Stewart, aka that internet audio guy. He challenged me to produce better interviews using better gear. He also happened to sell that gear online. I purchased everything he had to sell, and to this day I represent a small percentage of people who actually took what he offered, applied it, and still successfully do it years later.

Mike and I became good friends, so it was only natural that I would reach out to him for advice. "Well, Son," he said in his thick Atlanta accent, "Can you say video?"

Video, or online television as he used to say, is going to be big, and you need to be doing it now. He said, "I'm doing a workshop in Atlanta. I want you to come down. Be my guest. You just have to get your hairy butt down here. We're going to teach you how to shoot and edit video."

I thought, "Cool, this is right on the cutting edge." My wife, Diane, and I went to Atlanta and joined Mike for his weekend workshop. There were 30 other people in the room, and what a diversity of skill sets! On one side of the room were people who thought a mouse was something you fed cheese. On the other side were guys who thought they were with the CIA and were trying to manipulate the orbit of satellites in space! There we were in the middle, basically wondering when it was time to leave. It really wasn't that bad, because I learned enough of the basics to actually start doing my interviews using a video camera instead of a microphone.

But publishing videos to the Web opened up an entire new host of challenges. YouTube was still in its infancy, as was Adobe Flash, and there was no easy-to-use tool yet available for taking a video from the desktop and magically publishing it to the Web for the world to see.

Well, a few months later Mike Stewart was hosting another live event in Atlanta, but this time his buddy Jim Edwards was presenting with him. There were two Internet marketing powerhouses under one roof, and I got a free ticket to attend!

I attended, along with about 300 other people, and lady luck must have been smiling upon me that day, because sitting at my table was the only fellow Canadian in the room. This man, Shawn Pringle, became my new friend. It turned out he was a bit of a mad inventor and Internet marketer and had developed one of the first easy-to-use software programs to quickly convert your video to Flash and upload it to the Web. It was called V2F, and it was exactly the solution I was looking for—something easy to use that uploaded video fast!

During the following years, we collaborated, and V2F eventually grew into a robust video marketing/hosting solution with cutting-edge features, but it remained true to its motto: No geek required. Today Shawn and I are partners in what we now call EasyWebVideo.com.

With over 7,000 customers, we have become one of the leaders in the video hosting/marketing space. It's been an exciting ride, and we're only getting started!

About the Author

Michael Krisa has a unique style that demystifies video marketing and helps entrepreneurs and small businesses implement this powerful new strategy into their marketing mix.

Michael is a licensed real estate broker, a syndicated columnist, and a freelance Internet marketing consultant.

As a sought-after speaker and trainer, he is best known for helping people use video and video marketing in a way that actually works to make them money!

They say that the proof is in the pudding. Well, in July 2014, Easy Web Video was the #1 selling product for the day, #1 for the week, and #3 for two months on JVZoo.com.

Michael's subsequent product release, Email Click Magnet, debuted on JVZoo in November 2014, and it also took a turn as Product of the Day, with over 2,134 sales in the first four days.

His latest initiative is TabletVideoForAgents.com, a comprehensive online course that radically simplifies video making/editing and syndication by harnessing what he calls the all-in-one-video-solution…the iPad.

An avid skier and kayaker, Michael also plays the banjo!

You can enjoy Michael's work by visiting his blog, ThatInterviewGuy.com, or email him at michael@EasyWebVideo.com.

Connect with Michael on:

Facebook: facebook.com/michael.krisa

Michael Created:

It you are serious about using video for your marketing efforts and need a video player that engages your audience by providing clickable images, lead capture forms, web page templates, and video email, just to name a few…oh, and is easy to use…then you want EasyWebVideo.com.

We harness the power and security of Amazon S3 for your video hosting, plus the social media connectivity of Facebook, all at the click of your mouse.

Online since 2004, our motto says it all: Easy Web Video—No Geek Required.

Find out more at: EasyWebVideo.com

How To Ensure Your Product Is An Epic Fail

by Pat Flanagan

How to ensure your product is an epic fail

Most people in this book will tell you what to do. I'm going to be a bit different and tell you what <u>not</u> to do. Many simple and even common sense mistakes can turn a successful product into an epic fail. Every major product creator has committed at least one of these crimes, myself included. Follow these easy steps and you'll be sure to fail just like the rest of us!

Develop a product nobody wants···
When you're coming up with product ideas, be sure to totally ignore your market. Don't ask them what they're looking for or what problems they need to solve, just come up with a product idea that you fall in love with and run with it. After all, if you love it, there must be at least four other people out there who will love it as much as you do and will buy it, right? It's a start.

···Or develop a product that "everyone" will want

On the other hand, you could forget about niche marketing and just develop a product that everyone will want. Then you can devote a massive marketing budget to reaching the mainstream, rather than an easily targeted group. If it works for Proctor & Gamble, you should be able to do the same thing by yourself. It can't be that hard.

Develop a product that doesn't do what you say it does···

You don't really think that people care that much about your product actually working, right? If you're launching software, don't bother testing it on multiple versions of Windows, or in conjunction with other software. If you're launching a money-making or traffic technique, if it makes sense to you, no need to actually put it into practice. Nobody really cares if it doesn't quite do everything you say it does.

···Or shoot for absolute perfection from the start

Don't release your product when it's just good enough. Be sure to spend at least a year, maybe two, tweaking your product to absolute perfection. That way, you can sell just as many units as you would have with a "good enough" product, while having a maximum time investment. You also won't have to worry about those pesky product updates, which give you a reason to contact your customers. They don't really want to hear from you after they purchase anyway.

Develop a low-priced front end product with no upsell funnel

Successful product creators will develop a high-priced product, then "divide and conquer" that high-priced product into a series of successively lower-priced products, building an upsell funnel in reverse. But why go to all that work? Just develop a self-contained low-priced product that has nothing to sell to buyers afterward. You shouldn't risk irritating one of your buyers by presenting them with additional offers that could automate your process, expand their profit potential, or teach/coach them to greater success. Especially forget about things like resale rights or private label rights. Those are just ways for you to make more money, which won't help you fail.

Develop a dead-end product with no possible follow-up products

If you're going to ignore upsells, then you should also ignore follow-up products, because they're another source of income. Don't develop a product that could have add-on expansion packs. Don't plan something like an every-three-month strategy of presenting your buyers with upgrades. Instead, make sure your product is a one-and-done dead end, so you can do the entire product development process every single time.

Who needs a list?

When you release your product, don't waste money on an autoresponder like GetResponse or Aweber. You don't need to maintain a list and you certainly don't want to risk annoying your buyers by sending marketing emails to them. Avoid that unnecessary income stream by forgetting to maintain a buyers email list. You don't need to contact them with any updates or upgrades anyway, right?

Set your price too low or too high

The best way you can fail against other product creators is by underpricing them. Whatever price they're charging, undercut them as much as possible. Who cares if you lose money with each sale, you can make it up in volume! Plus, you'll be helping train the marketplace to expect extremely low prices for everything. Why charge $47 when you can charge $27, or why charge $27 when you can charge $7, right? Hell, charge $4 instead of $7. After all, your product has no value.

But your product is amazing, isn't it? It's everything you love, right? Maybe you should price it as high as you can. If everyone else is charging $47 for their product, you should definitely charge $147, because your product is that much better. Why soil your product by having too many buyers getting their grubby hands on it?

Load your sales copy with BS…

When it comes time to write your sales copy, don't worry about keeping it truthful. Load it up with as much puffed up BS as you can. Who cares if you get a huge refund rate, at least you can say you made a big amount of sales up front. Be sure to do whatever you can to insult the intelligence of your potential buyers. Treating them like they're idiots is always a great way to end up with an epic fail.

···And trash your competition on your sales page

Don't forget to mention your competition on your sales page. Don't compare product features and benefits, though. Just get dirty and trash them. Don't mince words, put it all out there in no uncertain terms. When you badmouth your competition, you draw in the type of buyer who will trash the people they buy from at the drop of a hat. Birds of a feather flock together, so why not flock with the lowest birds possible.

Launch without affiliates or publicity···

Your product is so amazing, the buyers will beat a path to your door, right? That means you don't have to worry about affiliates. They just steal half your profits, anyway. Just "build it and they will come." You don't need a network like JVZoo…in fact, why are you reading this book? You're so much smarter than that.

You also don't need to waste time on any launch publicity. Don't bother listing your site on websites like MunchEye, or on the many Facebook and Skype groups devoted to affiliate marketing and launch publicity. It's just a waste of time because you aren't going to be pushing for affiliate partners anyway.

···Or announce your product the day before you launch

Who cares that major affiliates have their promotions booked up weeks, or even months, in advance? They'll still drop everything they're doing and back out on their previous agreements, just so they can promote your work of art. You're going to rock the world with this product and everyone knows it. You can expect the whole market to screech to a halt.

Make sure at least seven other major product sellers are launching the same day you are

This falls in with not needing affiliates or publicity. You will obviously prevail by launching on a day when other major launches are occurring. The more, the better—bring it on, because competition doesn't concern you. The teeming masses are awaiting your product with baited breath (even though you haven't publicized it). They'll definitely ignore the other launches going on and zero in on yours. Just drop your product on the market, with no concern for what else is launching that day or week. How could it fail?

Launch with ridiculous prizes you can't afford or affiliates can't win

If you do decide to allow affiliates the supreme privilege of promoting your product, be sure you load up your launch with overblown prizes to entice them. Give away a car for promoting your $7 product. That'll make the affiliates line up to promote your launch. You'll be sure to get a flood of fraudulent sales from people who will run with the prizes, while you get stuck with the refunds and chargebacks. Being upside down on the prize cost versus profits isn't that big a deal.

Of course, you could wimp out and mitigate that risk by putting unreachable sales minimums in place. Make your affiliates sell at least 500 units before qualifying for a prize. Who cares if there are only a few affiliates who can move that many units, and the rest will just snicker when they see the minimums? Your product is going to crush it, right?

You've got to be kidding!

I hope you've keyed in on the sarcasm contained in this chapter. You obviously don't want your product to be an epic fail…you want epic success! But hearing what <u>not</u> to do is as important as hearing what you <u>should</u> do. Absorb both sides of the equation and you'll be ten steps ahead in your quest for success!

About the Author

Pat Flanagan designed his first website in 1996 for his corporate employer. Soon after, he left to fly solo, designing websites for his own clients. During this time, Pat started dabbling in e-commerce with his own websites. Fast forward to today, when Pat is helping others become successful online, while still developing and marketing products of his own. His deep well of experience in graphic design, copywriting, product funnel development and branding, backend product delivery construction, and affiliate recruiting makes Pat a one-stop concierge for getting your product off the shelf (or just plain finished) and into the market.

Connect with Pat at:

CreatorCare.com

Facebook: facebook.com/patlflanagan

Pat Created: PRPowershot.com

Ideas That Stick

by Dan Anton

You're making how much online?!" That was the disbelieving question my parents asked me in 1995 after I finished setting up my very first website. At the age of 15 my web design knowledge was extremely limited, but I managed to put together a website that sold hard-to-find video games. It was essentially an arbitrage system in which I purchased video games from Funcoland and marked them up for sale online. I didn't get wealthy and retire from this, but it was still profitable, and more importantly, it got me hooked on being an entrepreneur.

I repeated the process of making money online throughout college by selling various e-books and guides on eBay. I studied computer programming and marketing, which I felt were essential skills in the areas that interested me the most. I was falling in love with being my own boss, but this was not my first love. It was my second.

On September 11, 2001, I looked out my college dorm window and saw something that would alter my path forever. The World Trade Center Twin Towers were on fire and I, like everyone else, was in complete shock. Without any reservations, I decided to join the Army to become an officer and lead men in combat. It wasn't because I wanted revenge or had a love of war; it was because my first love is leading and serving. I knew I had the ability to lead men into combat and save lives. What began as a bold decision soon felt more like a duty from which I could not turn away.

Before I even arrived at basic training, I set goals for myself. I wrote them down to be reminded of these promises.

1. To join the infantry as an officer, where I could best lead men by my example.
2. To become an Airborne Ranger.
3. To successfully lead men in combat and make a difference.
4. To ascend to the rank of General.

If you are going do so something, you should give it everything you have or don't bother doing it at all. That is the core philosophy for how I live my life. I believe goal-setting is vital to everything. If you go into something with the attitude that you will not come away from it without success, then you cannot lose.

That was exactly the attitude I embraced before entering Ranger school, which has a graduation rate of less than 50 percent. This statistic is all-too-familiar to potential Ranger school students, who already know that less than one percent of the entire Army is Ranger-qualified.

During my first deployment to Iraq, I realized I had already obtained my first three goals. The third goal was achieved through some of the worst conditions a human being can face. Many of these conditions are portrayed in The Gods of Diyala, a book that features me in some of these situations. The fourth goal was long-term, since it would take awhile to make General from First Lieutenant.

Nevertheless, I was extremely satisfied with where I was in life because I'd discovered that I truly enjoy helping others improve themselves. Being an army officer is a lot like being a motivator and manager, but in the most extreme conditions. You have to lead by example even when you are tired, cold, and emotionally challenged from watching your brothers in arms being killed in front of you. One of my soldiers remarked to me, "Sir, I would follow you into hell." Of course, that was never an objective I was planning, but it demonstrates the impact one can have on someone else's life. My decision to make the Army my career had nothing to do with politics and everything to do with inspiring my men to be the very best that they could be.

Unfortunately, sometimes goals and reality don't match. During my second deployment, I suffered a combat injury to my lower spine, which would change the course I was so intent on pursuing. I struggled to rehabilitate my back for over a year before doctors recommended I be medically discharged. This was the lowest point of my life. I was about to be out of a job, but even worse, I was losing my identity. And, to add insult to injury, I was going through a divorce.

I would be lying if I said I wasn't feeling sorry for myself at that time. I had dark days when I wanted to give up and blame the world for my problems. But then I reached a point when I made a conscious decision to not take a single step backwards.

I started channeling my inner entrepreneurial spirit by brainstorming ideas by the hundreds. I wrote them down and eliminated ones that were no good... and there were plenty of them! One idea that stuck with me was an idea to create a social network for gamers.

I asked my brother, Matt Anton, to partner with me in this venture. Matt handled all the marketing while I focused on development and community. The beta version of the site was a huge success, drawing close to 10,000 members within the first few months. It was difficult to generate revenue at such an early stage, however, and Matt had bills to pay. Fortunately, he was able to leverage his newfound Search Engine Optimization (SEO) knowledge to land a marketing job for a major travel agency. Unfortunately, this meant I had to hire an SEO company to continue trying to rank our growing website.

During this point I was transitioning out of the Army, but I still had clerical work to do for my unit. Any spare time I had was spent learning about SEO so I could do the work myself and save some money in the process. I committed myself to learning everything and anything on the subject. For probably at least a month I slept only three hours a night because my appetite for success outweighed my need for sleep.

But sometimes life has to kick you down more than once to make sure you really want something. I awoke one morning to find my website had been penalized in Google because of bad SEO practices used by the company I'd hired. I was devastated, but for some reason I knew that everything was going to be okay and I didn't give it a second thought.

My ambition had never been more energized and laser-focused than at that particular time in my life. I immediately started building niche websites and optimizing them with what I had taught myself. Within the first month I had about a dozen sites, each making a few bucks a day through AdSense. I was thrilled to see my plan come together in the form of passive income.

As I continued my online education, I started to notice huge voids that were begging to be filled by software and services with an emphasis on simplicity. My ideas notebook was soon filled with my brainchild—what would become BacklinksIndexer.com. Backlinks Indexer was the culmination of everything I had learned with regards to how to rank higher by making backlinks more powerful.

It encompassed so many different moving parts that I needed help. I asked Matt to leave his job and partner with me so we could help website owners succeed online. We wanted to help others so they were not victims of poor SEO practices like we once were. It wasn't long before Backlinks Indexer gained the attention and accolades of top marketers in the SEO community. I am very proud that BacklinksIndexer.com is still the #1 rated indexing service, used by thousands of members and integrated with hundreds of software platforms. It is now available on JVZoo, where new affiliates are thrilled to promote such a beneficial product.

Success started to snowball as we continued to release more and more software services that the community embraced with open arms. Six months after my last day in the Army, my business was comprised of four different software services and generated over one million dollars in revenue. But the best part for me was getting emails from customers thanking me for their online success.

How was I was able to succeed in spite of numerous setbacks? What secret did I know? It was the very same principle that kept me going through Ranger school, and through the worst things imaginable on a deployment—sheer will! You have to know without a shadow of a doubt that you will succeed. If you don't truly believe that you will be successful, then why even bother at all? I didn't get the chance to make General, but I did leave the Army as a Major. I still get to impact lives for the better, but in a much different way than I ever imagined.

About the Author

Dan Anton is a lifelong entrepreneur with a passion for leading and serving. He created his first website in 1996 at the age of 16. After graduating college with honors, Dan decided to join the Army immediately following 9/11. Dan ascended to the rank of Major as an Infantry Ranger and served two combat tours for which he was awarded two Bronze Star Medals. An unfortunate combat injury forced Dan to leave his first love of serving his country and return to the entrepreneurial world. It wasn't long before Dan created a series of software products and services with his business partner and brother, Matt Anton. Within six months of being medically discharged from the Army, Dan's online business made just over one million dollars and continues to grow.

Connect with Dan at:

DanAnton.com

Facebook: facebook.com/daniel.b.anton.3

Twitter: @_DanAnton

LinkedIn: linkedin.com/in/dananton/

Dan Created:

BacklinksIndexer.com is the #1 Rated Backlink Indexing Service for over four years. BLI is used by over 10,000 members and hundreds of software developers that integrate directly with the software. Backlinks Indexer makes URLs 100 times more powerful by indexing and boosting them so that they help increase SERPs. Dozens of independent case studies consistently show BacklinksIndexer.com beating out the competition by a landslide.

Part 1: Simple Lessons From My Father

by Barry McLawhorn

Simple, Priceless Lessons from Childhood
Produce Infinite Value and Wealth

I grew up as the son of a modest small town preacher across a series of small towns in the southwestern Virginia mountains. Many times the subtlest actions or gestures of our parents change our lives forever (often in magical ways that we could never imagine—for better or worse).

I stretched lazily under the warmth of the quilt lovingly hand-crafted by my grandmother. I dozed beneath the heavy quilted fabric covered in a variety of hunting dogs including Pointers, Labrador, Irish Setters and more.

In the wonderland of my dreams I imagined a distant and disembodied voice, but it became more insistent and I slowly recognized my fathers, strong, gentle voice filled with a strange mixture of tenderness and authority as he said "Barry…Barry…Barry?"

My Dad's Simple Lesson:

My father said in a very firm and authoritative voice, "Get Up—I have something very important to teach you today."

I protested briefly, but to anyone who knew my father, it was obvious that my resistance was futile and the debate was over.

Other than when I had done something wrong that I knew would result in a vigorous spanking, I had never heard that urgency and purpose in my father's voice.

Sure that we were about to embark on an exciting adventure, I rushed behind my father's quick steps and said, "Where are we going?"

As I waited hungrily for his answer I began to let my mind wander to the pleasures I enjoyed with my Dad. Maybe we were going fishing—but we have no fishing rods. Maybe we were going to see the Indian skeletons in the archeological dig again.

I heard as my father called me "Come stand by the fireplace with me."

In childlike rebellion I wailed "Whyyyyyyyyy?"

Dad said proudly—"This a very important, I am going to teach you to shake hands."

"What do you mean? You are a preacher. I see you shake hands every Sunday and all the time. I already KNOW how to shake hands," I announced as I stuck my small chest out proudly.

Wisely my Dad said, "No. Son, today I am going teach you the art of shaking hands like a real Man." He emphasized the word "man" firmly and now I was intrigued.

He placed one strong hand on my shoulder and I felt the surge of something in his touch.

Dad said, "Now hold out your hand and shake my hand."

Enthusiastically I proclaimed "Okay!" But my body was not quite as awake as my mind and I halfheartedly placed a semi-relaxed hand in my father's own massive hand.

"That's pretty good, you took my hand, and you gripped it somewhat, but you did not look into my eyes Looking into a person's eyes immediately before your hands meet is the most important part of a handshake—it conveys an invitation and trust that is important for creating a first impression" he patiently explained.

I looked deeply into my Dad's eyes wondering what else he was about to reveal. I thought quietly to myself, "I never realized that my eyes were involved in a handshake." As I pondered this mystery my father's booming voice interrupted my thoughts.

"You look directly into a man's before you reach for his hand. Now let's practice this. Look directly into my eyes intently and reach for my hand."

Embarrassed and a bit confused I was afraid to look directly into my father's eyes because he towered above me and I knew if I made any mistakes he could be unforgiving. My father missed nothing and he noticed my hesitation immediately and barked—"I said look directly into my eyes."

I reached deep inside and gathered the courage to face my father as a man as an "equal" for the very first time. I felt older, wiser, and just plain weird. I pulled back my shoulders (like a man) and looked directly into the Dad's eyes seeing and appreciating him in a new way.

He was so, big, so strong, and so anchored—he looked like a statue. I looked directly into his eyes and thrust out my hand smiling shyly. He returned my look and my smile with a warm, glowing look of approval.

Now with both of his hands, my father took my right hand and cupped it between his calloused hands. Slowly he slipped his hand into mine until his thumb locked firmly against mine. With his other hand he brushed my brow and said, "This is how your hand should be when you shake hands. Do you feel the pressure against your thumb?"

"Yes Sir," I replied (another of Dad's unforgettable lessons was that I was always to say "Yes Sir" and "No Sir" or "Yes Ma'am" and "No Ma'am" when answering anyone older than I was. This was a non-negotiable demand from my father). Even forgetting momentarily was sure to incur his wrath, which meant at the very least a stern "mean look" and a harsh reminder.[1]

"Now look into my eyes and reach for my hand. Thrust your hand forward with authority until our thumbs lock firmly."

We practiced this simple motion at least 100 times. When I got it right my father beamed and praised me liberally. Any minor mistake in this "art" was met first with a gentle rebuke and then, an encouraging correction.

I focused on my Dad's lesson and example:

- Look directly into the other person's eyes.
- Thrust your hand forward with authority and confidence.

- Meet the other person's hand firmly until your hands lock at the base of your thumbs.
- Close your fingers, wrapping them firmly (but not painfully).
- Shake several times and nod your head slightly up and down (as if saying yes).
- Release hands, take a step back.
- Smile again as you look into the person's eyes.
- Continue to look deeply into the person's eyes as you listen intently to what they have to share with you.
- After hours of practice I was getting pretty good as this.
- Just then Dad said, "Now when you meet a Lady or and elderly person who may not be as strong as you are then there are some different rules just as there are when someone does not shake your hand properly."[1]
- Dad again used my hand as he demonstrated how to shake hands with an elderly person or someone with arthritis as he explained, "You do not hold or squeeze their hand as firmly because you do not want to cause them pain."
- "You never initiate a hand shake with a Lady, it is just not gentlemanly."
- A Lady (my father taught me that the word Lady should always be capitalized, especially if you were referring to "Your Lady") this was a symbol of the Southern respect, honor, and dignity my father held toward the "fairer sex."
- If a Lady extends her hand to shake your hand, Dad explained, "You hold her hand more gently and tenderly and sometimes you may lightly rest you other hand on the back of her hand very softly. You hold her hand this way until she begins to release your hand."

After hours Dad was finally satisfied. I had absorbed the lessons he so diligently sought to share with his "young man" that day and he said—"OK go find your Mom and let's get something to eat.

Somehow on that day something changed deep inside of me...I felt like a "Man" or at least that is what I thought I felt.

Today as a result of my Dad's loving "simple lessons" and the wisdom he shared with me from classic books like "How to Win Friends and Influence People" and "Influence" I live in a constant "Attitude of Gratitude" and I share this story as often as I can to express my gratitude for my father's wise training and to share the wealth (both tangible and intangible) that this simple lesson has created in my life.

References and Resources:
1   Etiquette In Society, In Business, In Politics And AT HOME—
    Emily Post. 1922
2   How to Win Friends and Influence People—Dale Carnegie, 1936
3   Influence: How and Why People Agree to Things—Robert B. Cialdini,
    1984

Part 2: Simple Lessons From My Mother

by Barry McLawhorn

MY MOTHERS SIMPLE LESSON:

f you are like me you remember the gentle (or not so gentle insistence) to always use the magic words "Please" and "Thank You!"

About the time I was 6 my parents threw my very first birthday party. It was a magical day. All my friends were there. My basement was filled with laughter and screams of joy from the sea of children.

We played pin the tail on the donkey and I actually pinned the tail in exactly the right point on the board.

The day was a swirling magical carousel of colors, laughter, and cake!

Hours later one by one my friends left and my mother said, "Barry you need to walk over to each parent and friend and thank them for your gift."

I said "Mrs. Valach thank you for bringing Mike to my party I really appreciate it and thank you Mike for giving me that great set of Hot Wheels cars. You'll have to come back so we can race against each other and watch the cars go trough the twin loops!"

Finally my last friend had left.

I gazed at the presents and had just decided what to play with first.

I heard my mother's voice say firmly—"Come here Barry!" There was a timbre to her voice I did not dare ignore. Because I knew as my Dad would whisper in my ear "You do not want to upset your mother."

Reluctantly I put down the cool multi-colored laser gun (that made noise, shot colored sparks, and smelled kind funny) to see what my mother wanted.

Mom took a small box off the bookcase shelves. I recognized it was those little cards that people send each other that are much smaller than an envelope and often bear the words "Thank You"– silly cards I thought to myself.

Mom again commanded "Sit Down" as her hand pushed down on my shoulder and made my compliance a non-issue. My little butt landed firmly on the hard kitchen chair that served as my Dad's executive chair.

Mom put first card in front of me and slipped a pen into my hand. "Barry, you need to write a thank you note to all of the people who gave you gifts."

I took the pen and sloppily scribbled two words, "Thank You" on the card and my efforts were barely legible (because I could not "write pretty" then either). Some things truly never change. ;-)

My mother said, "The first thing you must do is write the person's name who gave you the gift at the top of the card followed by a comma."

"Then you thank them for what they gave you."

So I wrote "Mike," and paused…

On the next line I wrote "Thank you so much for the great Hot Wheels cars—especially the Red Baron."

I struggle to write with the pen and it takes about three tries. Each time I messed up, Mom just hands me another card and I start again.

Finally I have a neatly, a properly completed thank you card that read:

Dear Michael,

Thank you so much for the cook Hot Wheels cars—especially the really neato Red Baron.

You'll have to come back soon so we can race each other!

Love,

Barry

I was never sure why, but my mother always wanted me to sign my letters, "Love, Barry." To this day I think it's weird.

"OK, grab the cards and let's go to the post office."

"Do we have to do it nooooowwww, Mom?"

Mom patiently replied, yes we must do it now. It's very important to thank someone as soon as you possibly can after they give you a gift. So, let's go!

Leveraging Your Business With a "Digital Handshake"

I've leveraged technology and the Internet, since before the birth of social media.

Remember the story about my mother teaching me the fine art of strengthening relationships by saying "Thank You" and sending Thank You notes.

I created what I call my "**Digital Handshake**."

A "Digital Handshake" is composed of 7 primary components:

1. A highly personalized subject line that includes "From Barry," the addressee's first name, and sentence fragment that asks a partial question.
2. The addressee's first name (coupled with a mutually shared familiarism like "Dude, Hey, RockStar, etc.).
3. The subject line is repeated as the first sentence in the e-mail message and the thought is completed.
4. The precise reason for the e-mail clearly stated.
5. What is In It for ME? (From the reader's point of view).
6. Social proof (i.e., Jason Mangrum, Brian Solis, Mike Filsaime, and Bryan Zimmerman Co-Founder of JVZoo.com have already said "yes" to this idea).
7. A laser focused call to action (such as "I will setup a time to introduce you to Gina Gaudio-Graves one-on-one to explore how we can best leverage everything we do with Directions University.")

The "Digital Handshake" Always Has 3 Additional Unique Features:

1. The closing is always personalized with either the phrase I use in business closings ("Very truly yours"), in a specific close personal relationship ("Namaste"), or directly related to the addressee in our personal communication ("Live Long and Prosper").

2. A smiling professional head shot (O.K., I am not smiling in mine, but I have been criticized for that and people have told my that my intensity makes me appear unapproachable—and has in fact cost me business! So, I highly recommend that you have a sincere glowing "smile from the eyes" in your signature section.

3. A direct "Call to Action" inviting the reader to "**Connect with Me**" listing every way possible to "reach out to me" and do business immediately:
   a. Telephone Number(s)
   b. Private Cell Number (for those who deserve the access)
   c. LinkedIn Profile Direct Link
   d. Facebook Profile Direct Link
   e. Twitter Handle Direct Link
   f. Skype ID
   g. Fax Number
   h. Optional Mailing Address(es) (Since I have this on my LinkedIn profile and LinkedIn in my primary source of referral and leads—I do not clutter my signature section with addresses).

Five Easy Ways To Leverage The Impact Of Your Digital Handshake:

1. State the benefit to the reader first and in short clear language.
2. Include a video or **VIDEOMAIL**[1] in your e-mail.
3. Include a **VThanks**.[2]
4. Subtly include a link to something that adds value to the reader's life, relationships, and or business(es).
5. Include a Suggested Deadline for their Response (ideally a deadline set by a 3rd party).

One Final Helpful Tip and a Gift For You:

Always say "Thank You" and offer acknowledgement and psychic rewards for each and every response from the recipient.

As I was writing this I had an additional relationship, business, and profit building secret I truly wanted to share with you, but my space here is limited, so if you would like to receive a personal e-mail from me with a real sample of the "Digital Handshake" and revealing my other secret, please click on this link http://www.marketingthatworks.TV/secret/

Thank you for taking time to hear my story and may you always exceed your ultimate outcome!

Very truly yours,

Barry C. McLawhorn

(404) 964—6595

Skype: MarketingThatWorks.TV

References and Resources:

1 VIDEOMAIL—http://www.marketingthatworks.tv/videomail

2 VThanks—http://www.marketingthatworks/vthanks

About the Author

Connect with "The Sterling Silver Strategist", Barry C. McLawhorn (http://www.MarketingThatWorks.TV/bio). Barry C. McLawhorn is the Founder of BedRock Viral Marketing & Associates, MarketingThatWorks.TV (Internship and Apprenticeship) and other marketing and "customer getting" businesses. In the non-profit area Barry is the founder of Americas Business Networking Group (http://www.meetup. com/ATL-AmericasBusinessNetworkingGroup/) and Boot Strap America.

Barry entered the Internet Marketing world in 1994. He has helped clients in the home mortgage business, the software industry, the professional IT and corporate training field, and the non-profit sector generate millions of dollars in additional sales using technology and influence psychology. Creator of "The Digital Handshake" he has used his "permission, access, and profit" philosophy to meet, connect with, interact with, and professionally interview thought leaders such as Brian Solis, Robert Cialdini, and the founders of Digital Capital Week (http://dcweek2011.sched.org/event/78f557e8fe32e57a88f74997d9324e59#).

Barry was also one of the first to monetize the Internet for automobile dealers and in 1999 increased his first auto dealership client's Internet lead generation by 900% and sales by 300% in less than 60 days.

Barry recently launched his first campaign on JVZoo.com for a client in the video and marketing automation software business by hosting a Marketer's Red

Carpet Event with Denise O'Brien of Dome Entertainment, LLC (a Hollywood public relations powerhouse) during Marketing Mayhem 2014. He attracted over 30 major marketers including Daven Michaels, Willie Crawford, Heather Vale, and Johan Mok from his sphere of influence just by messaging them on his Facebook account in the middle of the night. The silent pre-launch promotion for MaxLeadPRO 2-Way VIDEOMAIL, VIDEOTEXT, and marketing automation system generated nearly 50 sales for a $497 recurring subscription sale through JVZoo.com in the first pre-launch webinar and converted at nearly 10%.

Today, Barry serves as the Integration Marketing Specialist and Affiliate Development Manager for Directions University http://www.askggg.com/bedrockatv, MaxLeadPRO, and other businesses. He is a leading authority on creating and growing businesses (both on-line and off-line) through lead generation, e-mail marketing, social media and influence psychology.

Barry choses to work with "capable, competent, crusaders," (people who want to make a difference and change the world and builds his networks primarily through http://linkedin.com/barrycmclawhorn, http://facebook.com/barry.mclawhorn, https://twitter.com/mktgthatworkstv and by interviewing the worlds thought leaders and publishing their exciting tips, tools, and strategies on authority blogs and other media. Connect with Barry!

How I Failed My Way To Success

by Mitch Carson

N o matter how many times I felt knocked down, I always sucked it up, breathed deeply, raised my hands and spirit, and charged forward. Allowing myself to be knocked out was never an option.

How I failed my way to success

Our history defines who we are today. Experiences shape our personalities and the decisions we make. After an acrimonious divorce and all the financial and emotional effects, I had to make some life choices to steer my career in a different direction. Due to the divorce settlement and legal fees, I was forced to sell the advertising agency I had owned for 14 years. I began the business in my home and grew it to a multiple seven-figure agency with 17 employees. I had worked six or seven days a week for many years, living, breathing, and loving my business. It was a greater loss than divorcing my wife.

I was at a crossroads in my career. Emotionally I felt deflated. Financially I was diminished. But I was in the fortunate position of having lots of experience marketing various businesses. Being the inside expert for my previous clients was what gave me confidence for my next venture.

I decided to go fully online with my businesses and leave behind the office with all the overhead and issues associated with employees. My ears and eyes were opened when I heard and saw many others with less experience making a lot of money online. I wanted the same results and was willing to learn how to do it.

I had been watching people make money from AdSense and affiliate products. This required solid SEO skills and discovering the whole world of Internet traffic. I wondered how to get traffic targeted to my sites.

I decided to buy a piece of the puzzle. I started to buy websites on Flippa like they were crack. I was caught up in the rush of bidding and winning the bids. I was hooked on buying these purported money-making sites. I bought 40 of them in less than a month and sold stocks from my retirement accounts to feed my addiction.

It was then I realized I had a lot of work ahead of me. Oh boy, was I in over my head! I had no system and did not carefully check the traffic and income claims. I was completely screwed by unscrupulous sellers and conmen. Flippa does not vet the sellers well, and I was seriously ripped off. I was out of money, scared, and depressed.

But I had to dig myself out of the mess I'd created, so I got serious. I went on a furious search for fact versus fiction online. Prior to going 100% online, my expertise was direct mail. This knowledge and experience provided some help in marketing and copy, but it wasn't enough. I was like a trained boxer who entered the new world of mixed martial arts. I had only some of the skills necessary to survive and press forward.

The hardest part

To move forward, first I had to forgive myself for all the mistakes I'd made getting where I was. I spent well over six figures on websites that did not perform according to sellers' claims, and I was without an income. I felt ashamed and embarrassed. I have never before told anyone this story; the shame was too great.

But my drive to persevere came from knowing others had been there and have succeeded. If others did it, I could too. My background was martial arts, and in my years as an instructor, I tied over 700 black belts on students' waists. I taught that you must get up when you are knocked down. It is perfectly okay to be knocked down, but you must get up and go at it again. Life is an opponent at times. Get up, face it, and keep pressing forward with your momentum and inertia. The power of the spirit and intentions are greater than any opponent you create in your mind or in your path.

Helping others is the reward

When I can teach others to avoid my mistakes, I feel like I have achieved my purpose in life. I discovered the pitfalls of an online business and have been able to develop a system for vetting sites before I buy them or recommend them to clients. It includes a great tool called PR Powershot, which searches for aged domains that provide instant quality links and traffic to sites I owned. These two techniques revolutionized my business and renewed my confidence from a feeling of worthlessness and stupidity.

The most inspiring transformation

Making money while I sleep was my ultimate goal and manifestation. I get to live, work, and thrive anywhere in the world, with the only condition being a good Internet connection. When I found the tools and techniques that supported my objective, I felt relief. It was like receiving my diploma after four long years of college.

Having financial freedom and control over my income has given me my life back. I no longer feel handicapped and stupid. There are systems for growing a business online and great tools for knowing how to buy right and sell even higher. The skills I gained through trial and error, combined with an automated system to minimize time invested and provide accurate information, have led me down the path toward success.

About the Author

Mitch Carson is a published author (The Silent Salesman) and a former syndicated radio show host with CBS in Los Angeles. He has spoken on direct marketing in 11 countries, in both English and Spanish. He is responsible for nine-figure sales on television via infomercials and has been published in over 600 newspapers and magazines worldwide, ranging from the <u>Wall Street Journal</u> to the Sydney Morning Herald and Entrepreneur magazine, as well as CNBC News Television.

Mitch has had the good fortune of experiencing multiple business failures and successes, endured a five-year heated divorce from his attorney ex-wife, overcame health challenges, and is a serial entrepreneur who never gives up. Having earned a sixth-degree black belt, Mitch attributes his relentless drive and fortitude to literally being punched and kicked in the face thousands of times. On the professional karate circuit, pain forces change to whatever was not working. Applying this metaphor to business and life has enabled Mitch to push through every obstacle life has presented.

Connect with Mitch at:

MitchCarson.com

Facebook: facebook.com/mitch.carson1960

Twitter: @mitchellcarson

LinkedIn: linkedin.com/in/mitchcarson/

Mitch Created:

PR Powershot (www.prpowershot.com) is the only 100% automatic solution that grabs high page rank, massive-value expired domains for pennies on the dollar. It completely automates searching and bidding so you can build your portfolio in minutes.

INTRODUCING

Success By Connecting With Energy

by Bevan Bird

I filmed myself free solo climbing in skate shoes as I explained what I was doing. At one point, I got scared. I froze up. I was in a position where it was hard to make the next move, and I began shaking because I'd stopped flowing. It felt difficult to move back to my previous position, too. I realized that unless I got going again, I'd soon shake myself off the holds and it would be a long tumble down on sharp rocks. I wouldn't look pretty afterwards. I knew I had to stop being scared and either climb back or keep going, so I calmed myself down and climbed across that exposed section to safety.

That difficult moment made me realize I can control my mind. My friends' reactions to the YouTube video made me realize even more clearly how limited people's perceptions are of what we can and cannot do. Breaking the norms and then conquering my fear set me on a path of conscious awakening.

When climbing I had to focus entirely on the move I was making. Everything disappeared except what I was doing—I lost myself in my art. I found peace in the present moment.

I was working as an engineering surveyor at the time, and when the highway project paused for the winter, I went on seasonal layoff and got EI (the Canadian equivalent of unemployment benefits). It was the first time in five years that I had a significant amount of free time on my hands. I would seize the opportunity to change my life for the better!

I wanted to build a side income so I could have a better lifestyle and the freedom to live as I choose. As far as business is concerned, I've always wanted to do something that matters, something I believe in and that brings me joy in the moment. Plus, I want whatever I create to be useful for a long time, preferably forever. After reading two library books (stories of how the highest trafficked websites in the world, Google and Facebook, started), I decided on Internet marketing as my method.

Before making the change, I needed to reflect on my desired lifestyle and purpose. I have always felt connected with the universe. I suspected that my thoughts influenced reality, but kept this secret from others. In January 2010 I discovered the "Law of Attraction," which affirmed what I already knew. So I thought about what I wanted to create in my life: I wanted to travel the world, climb in beautiful places, make inspiring films, and talk with interesting people. That covers lifestyle, but what about purpose? Well, in my story, my clarity of purpose comes much later.

When I went back to work in surveying the next season, I saw clearly that my job was forcing me to do work that did not align with my values and beliefs. I didn't believe in contributing to destruction of the environment—I wanted to contribute to creation and inspiration instead. I realized I had forsaken my creative self by doing that work. Plus I had seen that there were better things out there. I quit in June 2010 with only $4,000 in my bank account.

I obviously needed to build my Internet marketing business quickly. Over the course of the next few years, I would experience many aha! moments that would change my life and get me where I am now, living comfortably in this 26th floor luxury apartment overlooking Stanley Park—according to TripAdvisor, "The best park in the world."

My first marketing client was a yoga teacher for deaf people. In the spring of 2011, I hosted my first live workshop on how yoga teachers could differentiate and work together to fill their classes more easily with social media.

But I built my business too slowly and made the mistake of selling on price instead of value. I didn't know about the power of expert positioning and high-ticket contrast offers. Long story short, I was evicted in the spring of 2011 with over $20,000 in debt. Thankfully my dad gave me a safe haven.

I then altered my approach slightly. I created my first social media course, a 400-page PDF to help small businesses get started on social media. I learned copywriting from Joseph Sugarman, Alex Mandossian, and others, and then a few people purchased it from my website. Lada Shabunina, a true fan of my social media course, helped me market it on social media. She effectively attracted fans and customers for me. She was my first affiliate.

Next, I began running Facebook ads. Then Facebook changed its interface, and because I had included specific how-to's in the social media course, it became something I would have to maintain and update. What a hassle that would be! Living with my dad off the grid, with very limited access to the Internet each week, Facebook's change was the straw that broke the camel's back. I abandoned that product for the time being.

Some time later, when I was in a hopeless state, considering bankruptcy, I applied a lesson from The Law of Success by Napoleon Hill. In February 2013, I decided on one goal and focus—to receive $100,000 in the year 2013. I repeated my statements 12 times each day with feeling and took action each time. Within three weeks, I was offered a surveying job that paid much more than my previous one, I accepted it for the money, quickly repaid my debts totaling $30,000 and exceeded my earning goal for that year. To celebrate, I took a trip to Playa del Carmen for my first all-inclusive resort experience and climbed limestone barefoot over white sand at Tulum.

At JVZoo's Marketing Mayhem Live 2014 in Orlando, Florida, I finally met many marketers I've looked up to for years. Joel Comm, Armand Morin, and Mike Filsaime are a few who come to mind. Spending time with people of this caliber raised my vibration, and my other creative intentions are also coming true. I've talked with hundreds of interesting and amazing people since 2010, and the people I'm connecting with now are getting increasingly interesting.

Several aha! moments came after Marketing Mayhem. To get a specific client I had to clearly differentiate myself from others, which moved me in the right direction. I also learned from Jeffrey Gitomer's masterpiece The Little Red Book of Selling that selling is really creating an environment in which the customer feels comfortable buying.

In October 2014 I began working with my coach, Sean Mize, and quickly learned that you must know your purpose or you will not sell much. Once you know your purpose, it will free you to grow! But that's where I was stuck. I wasn't clear.

Then Sean's Two Hour Product Creation training moved me to action; I created my first screen capture video: a two-hour training on evaluating Facebook groups and the admins of those groups. I recorded myself joining the best JV groups I could find at the time. Feedback on that training: "Awesome stuff… Thank you."

I also did the work to find my purpose. Of course, at a simple level, like all humans, my purpose is joy. But I had to go further. What is it that I'm here to give to the world? How <u>specifically</u> am I designed to expand consciousness and happiness? I realized my most valuable ability is dealing with people. I go deeper and take it farther than what we've learned from Dale Carnegie (<u>How to Win Friends and Influence People</u>) and Stephen R. Covey (<u>The Seven Habits of Highly Effective People</u>).

By being consciously aware of my vibration and purposefully elevating it before and during communications, I engage with people energetically, resulting in powerful communications being received clearly. To take this to a higher level, first ask the Universe why it is bringing you together with this other person. People tell me they love my energy. I make people feel inspired and great! You can do this too and increase your high-ticket sales.

About the Author

Bevan Bird's mission is to support conscious expansion by assisting light tribes to band together more powerfully, so we can do even more amazing and wonderful things together in sustainable ways… so that ultimately humanity becomes even happier and more fulfilled and we can live more harmoniously in an even more wonderful, vibrant, abundant, creative atmosphere on Earth. He loves helping people connect energetically with their self and then with each other, from the heart.

Bevan Bird co-creates the High Vibrational Connecting trainings. He lives in Vancouver, BC, Canada.

Connect with Bevan at:
BevanBird.com
Facebook: facebook.com/birdify
Twitter: @birdify
LinkedIn ca.linkedin.com/in/birdify

Bevan Created:

Do you want to make a bigger impact? Do you want to collaborate with me or other light bearers so we can kick this multidimensional Love party up yet another notch?

Connect with your true self and love and accept yourself unconditionally. It will become easier to communicate energetically, attract and connect with just the right beings. I can help you do this.

Watch over my shoulder as I show you step-by-step exactly how I easily find and connect with leaders of conscious evolution and explore ways we can collaborate to fulfill our missions.

You can find this at: highvibrationalconnecting.com

Dreamers Are Winners

by Ali Gadit

A s I write this from my condo in lower Manhattan, I see fireworks bursting over the Statue of Liberty. This undeniable symbol of freedom is lit up by colorful, powerful explosions. It's not the Fourth of July, simply a Saturday in New York City.

These fireworks remind me of the freedom I've attained after transitioning out of the 9 to 5+ daily grind and the Wall Street hedge fund strongholds of the American finance industry. I long yearned for the freedom to be my own man, my own boss, and to fully love the life I was given as the first generation American son of immigrant parents. The symbolic nature of the fireworks outside my window strikes many chords with me, to say the least.

Nothing in life comes easy, as they say, and I've worked extremely diligently to get where I am, since I was a young boy growing up in the suburbs of Long Island, New York. My first job was the neighborhood paperboy. I would wake at an ungodly early hour before school and deliver the newspapers to my route's customers, making sure I'd be tipped handsomely for the service at the end of every week. Of course, this was well before the days of the Internet and touch-to-receive-updates we've come to know as today's norm.

My chrome GT Mach 1 bicycle shone in the early morning sun as I peddled hard to complete my route. The customary milk crate attached to the front of my bike held the newspapers I would chuck at people's homes. The bike route also provided a great way to get to know my neighbors. Once the winter snows fell on suburban Long Island, it was easy for me to ask the same neighbors to pay me to shovel their walkways and driveways. At that tender young entrepreneurial age and spirit, coming home with several hundred dollars and a sore back made it all worthwhile.

I was the son of two hard-working immigrant parents who did their best to provide my three siblings and me with all we needed, but financially, things were tight, to say the least. As the eldest of four children, I did my best to buy myself the things I needed that my parents simply couldn't afford, due to the competing priorities of a mortgage, property taxes, and all the other joys that come with pursuing the American Dream.

After my paperboy days were up, I became a licensed driver by the State of New York at the ripe age of 16. I used my saved tips to buy my first car, a 1987 Nissan Sentra. It was nothing special, but I got a taste of freedom—the ability to go from point A to point B in a reliable and safe manner. It opened me up to more opportunities: a Chock full o'Nuts coffee shop, Burger King, TGIF restaurant, and a boutique Mediterranean restaurant called Ayhan's Shish Kebab.

Soon, however, I moved on to working as a sales associate at a Banana Republic retail clothing store, the job that fit me best at the time. I enjoyed helping people match various garments and often surpassed my sales quota. It was truly a grind, but it also taught me the true nature of working in a mega-conglomerate corporation. And it didn't quell my entrepreneurial spirit, as I managed to also work as a promoter for a few Manhattan nightclubs. I always saw myself living in the Big Apple, and growing up with TV shows such as Seinfeld and Friends only fueled my desire to live there.

I was accepted to many colleges, but I settled on the University of Buffalo (SUNY) to pursue pharmacy school. It had just become a doctoral program, meaning it would take a minimum of six years to complete pharmacy school.

While attending classes and having plenty of fun, my entrepreneurial spirit persisted, and I connected with a premiere nightclub an hour away in Toronto. Every week I needed to provide busloads of college kids ready to spend their

American dollars at the type of establishment that the city of Buffalo couldn't offer. I made up to several thousand dollars a week doing that, which meant I didn't need to have a normal job while at school.

Instead of graduating with a Doctor of Pharmacy degree, as I initially set out for, I finished with a four year Bachelor's degree in biochemical pharmacology. Those years in upstate New York were truly magical and provided me the opportunity to learn from my studies and my new experiences, away from the sheltered life with my parents on Long Island.

After graduation in 2003, I decided to depart from everything I had studied and go big-time in the financial world. My gamble worked, as I became a banker with several firms and amassed enough money one year out of college to buy my first property—a piece of waterfront real estate on the sandy shores of Long Island at the age of 22! However, those banking days came to a sharp end shortly after, with the banking meltdown of 2007-2008. Out of work and broke, I managed to keep my property and arranged to work with a Long Island law firm as a banking consultant. I continued to thrive.

Throughout these years I had a relationship with a crazy beautiful blonde; the relationship brought to life my beautiful baby girl, Avianna. Since my life was taken to a whole new level as a new dad, I decided to start over, re-learn everything, and be a proprietary trader at T3 Capital, a Wall Street hedge fund.

This change allowed me to finally realize my dream of living and breathing in the concrete jungle—Manhattan. But it was also my most difficult job, as it was extremely high stress and required incredibly long hours. I just didn't find it fulfilling, and I felt an elephant standing on top of my freedom, stifling all creativity—not to mention killing any chance of quality time with my growing baby girl. I needed a dramatic change and fast, as I wasn't enjoying what I was doing at all.

One night, after watching the movie <u>The Social Network</u>, I had an aha! moment that inspired me to take things to a whole new level. I wanted to be in the digital space, as I knew that's where the future was. I could attain the American Dream much sooner on this route, rather than being a lemming in the corporate machine.

After doing major research and putting on my digital thinking cap, I submitted my resignation to Wall Street. It was risky, but I knew it would be the only way to give my all to this digital venture, to have success without that time suck, and to eventually have a life, for that matter.

Make it or break it, as they say! I first managed a couple digital brands as a JV manager, gaining a wealth of knowledge and connections in the process. This is when I learned about an emerging affiliate powerhouse platform called JVZoo. During this period of discovery, I realized I wanted to provide high-end software for Internet marketers all around the world.

I created my first company, Ali G. Marketing LLC. I connected with a high-level coder named Marcus Lim who worked in the same industry in Australia. I eventually brought him on as my full-time Chief Technology Officer. We share many interests and aspirations, so it was a business-minded match made in heaven.

I've finally attained a level of freedom I didn't think was possible. I work on my own terms and treat my team with respect, and we achieve the goals I set in a mutually beneficial way. I've launched my software products using the JVZoo platform, as it's an absolute hub of entrepreneurs who want to promote high-quality products. I have connected with so many others like me in the process. They have promoted my software, and I reciprocate to my 30k+ buyers list. My software has helped change lives from what was to what they never thought possible.

Since this career shift I feel that I'm truly beginning to live the American Dream my parents set out to provide and I can pass on to my lineage. Keep in mind, always go against the grain, do what your heart wants you to do, and please dream. Without dreams we really have nothing to look forward to. The dreamers and those who seek freedom in life are the actual winners.

About the Author

Ali G. is an Ex-Banker & Ex-Wall Street Hedge Fund Proprietary Trader, who's made a Dramatic & Successful transition to the field of Software Development for Internet Marketers all around the world.

Leaving the Wall Street world wasn't easy for him, yet does not miss that rat-race at all…!

Software solutions for Internet Marketing is what Ali G. has brought to the table since 2012. Giving them 'an Edge' that's never existed before, for the most effective use of Social Networks, especially such as Facebook and Twitter.

Ali G. Marketing is changing the lives of Businesses & Entrepreneurs everywhere and in the process accumulated countless positive testimonials of success by marketers using his highly-developed software.

You can connect with Ali at:

AliGMarketing.com

Twitter: @aligmarketing

Ali Created:

Facebook Data Extraction desktop software using the Facebook API to base Facebook Ads laser-targeting for Highly Successful campaigns.

Twitter Data Extraction desktop software using the Twitter API to base Twitter Ads laser-targeting for Highly Successful campaigns.

You can find the Facebook Data Extraction took at: AliGMarketing.com/Products

The Valuable List

by Lindsey Holmes

The Entrepreneur

stumbled upon my main JV product, FB Fever. I also stumbled upon JV marketing itself. I was chasing a business opportunity: buying premium domains.

I am a proud serial entrepreneur. I am also a technologist at my core and have been lucky and blessed to discover some golden geese in the dot-com age. I was there at the very beginning of the social media/social media marketing craze ten years ago, lending me thought leadership and loyal clients in my digital agency. I understood the power of the e-book early and have ridden the e-book wave, with over 11 books that continue to do well. I've also scored some lucrative domains that have netted me consistent money in many ways through the years.

So when I discovered the domain reseller bidding site Flippa, I was a kid in a candy store. I was particularly attracted to the social media-related domains, due to my field of expertise and passion but also the statistically high traffic to these domains. As the idea sets in that good ol' fashioned jobs might not be attainable and self-starting may the only way to go, smart entrepreneurs flock to social media tools and training to help them market their lean startups. My find was invigorating.

I immediately thought about some easy, continual streams for FBFever.com. Some simple SEO, or even just ads on a landing page might be lucrative. I thought about an e-book or a training course. FB Fever seemed like the perfect title for a guide to maximizing Facebook ad marketing, audience targeting, and leveraging my overall knowledge bank.

I hadn't even clicked the link yet, but I could imagine the vacations! And when I clicked, I would unleash a whole new world, a marketer's dream. JV marketing would infuse some energy into the saturated market of social media marketing, and it would add residual income I've spent years looking to solidify. It would also find me under the tutelage of some characters but solid entrepreneurs. Joel Comm, E. Brian Rose, Bryan Zimmerman, Todd Gross, and so many more continue to prove the value of hustle, reinvention, and the power of will.

The Click

That click…The listing for FBFever.com boasted a premium domain, a 36,000 Alexa rating, a turnkey 10-module video and written course complete with a membership plugin, $10,000 in revenue, validated daily income between $150-300 in its two-week run, and the promise of tutelage by a "Great" in the JV world. The latter was of little consequence to me, as I really had no clue what JV marketing was, but I did see value in learning whatever a great coach could teach me. I researched JV marketing on my own, but I discovered that the best way to learn was to jump in head first.

I weighed the risks, and as far as I was concerned, the 36,000 Alexa rating would allow me to do something with this purchase, even flipping it if I had to. A return on my investment would come within 4-6 months, based on calculations that factored the slowing of traffic after a launch. I even added in the possibility of a bout of entrepreneurial laziness. For a week the bidding was neck and neck, but I willed my win. I paid $9,500 for FB Fever in February 2014.

The Morning After

After the high on my win and 'yet another no brainer opportunity' (YANBO) settled down, I began to get a bad feeling in the pit of my stomach. I have been known to fall victim to buyer's remorse, but this felt a little different. This time it was my intuition, and she was smacking me dead in the face. It was only the morning after, but I was jarred by the lack of pings signifying PayPal deposit alerts in my email. They just weren't coming in. That day I made $18. The site had a consistent Flippa-validated $150-300 in income just yesterday!

My YANBO netted me $200 for the next two weeks. Then about $400 over the next two months, a far cry from the cash cow enterprise I thought I had purchased. I should also mention that the Alexa rating dropped with my traffic, and the "JV Great" who was going to teach me a thing or two went on an extended vacation. I was on my own, and unlike my original plan, it seemed unwise to scrap the really great content for ads. But the $9,500 I'd invested in the site was not disposable income for me, so I made up my mind to learn how to monetize my product and to understand the JV culture.

The Pivot: Use My List

Months later, after a ton of research and strategic outreach to key players in the field, I found that I already knew most of what I needed to know to jump-start sales. I had separated my digital marketing experience from JV marketing, overlooking some real value in the process.

I began to host seminars and target the course materials to my social media and traditional marketing clients. Sure, the landing pages and sales content can appear a little different for a JV launch, but marketing and sales are marketing and sales. I then discovered the one resounding commonality that would turn things around for my investment—The List!

Since purchasing FB Fever, I had been receiving inquiries for my suggestions for other similar or complementary products. I gave suggestions freely, and then my light bulb moment came. I could sell other products to my engaged list and receive commission through JVZoo and other affiliate programs. Brilliant! My first email blast netted me $1,000, and I realized there was real value in my list.

I incorporated my copywriting and social media marketing experience into my email blasts, delivering content that was engaging and went beyond swipes, giving my buyers access to a real human voice and building trust. My bi-weekly email blasts have since netted me over $30,000 in affiliate sales, surpassing my estimated return on investment.

My list also helped breathe new life into my product itself. My buyers are using the key lessons they've learned through Facebook marketing to promote my product and find their own success in JV marketing.

The Win

Initially I categorized my win as the return on my investment. Indeed it was. The greater win, however, has been discovering a whole new industry, learning to embrace the pivot, and understanding how to harness my current resources. I have found a niche in bridging the digital marketing and JV marketing worlds, and I'm passionate about creating a more seamless connection.

About the Author

Lindsey has used her writing, marketing, and business background, her self-taught programming skills, and her passion to empower through tech to become a key player in the Web 2.0 industry. She has authored five books, developed a Facebook marketing training course as well as the website FB Fever, and speaks on stages across the world.

Lindsey owns an award-winning digital marketing agency, and she is the Evernote Entrepreneurship Ambassador, a member of Delta Sigma Theta Sorority, Inc., an active alumna of the Madeira School and Sarah Lawrence College, and the mom of a Shih Tzu named Banks.

Connect with Lindsey at:

UsableTech.co

Facebook: facebook.com/usabletech

Twitter: @lindseycholmes

Lindsey Offers:

FB Fever is a monster all-in-one Facebook training course, complete with seven modules, each of which teaches a unique method of making money through Facebook marketing. It provides over 90 minutes of written and video training in each module.

Learn more at: FBFever.com

Seeing Double

by Ron Dowell

Every morning we wake up from the previous night's sleep. The quality of our sleep often sets the precedence for the day ahead. One particular morning was no exception for me.

I was about to turn 60, and I was enjoying my work helping local businesses market themselves online. I worked with them on developing their websites, programming applications, building databases, and even fixing their computers if something happened. I was the all-around tech guy for the area.

I woke up that morning and immediately knew something was seriously wrong. I was seeing double. It took everything I had to keep it together and not panic. I assumed that since there was something wrong with my vision, I should see the optometrist. The optometrist sent me straight to the emergency room in fear that I was having a stroke.

I saw several doctors in the emergency room and had a lot of tests. Several hours later the doctors also thought I'd had a stroke. A neurologist was called in to evaluate me. He thought the same but wasn't entirely sure because both sides of my body had been affected, which was not a typical outcome of a stroke.

Over the next three days, my body seemed to completely fall apart and shut down from the inside out. I lost most of my vision, my ears rang so loud I could hardly hear, and my speech became really slurred. I couldn't walk without the assistance of my wife and a walker.

I couldn't see what was going on around me. I could barely hear the concern in my wife's voice or even the questions the doctors were asking me. I couldn't even tell anyone how bad I felt all over. I had no way of knowing what was going on or any way to communicate what I felt inside. All I could do was sit or lay there and feel the intense confusion. I really thought I was dying.

After three days, I stopped getting worse and very slowly started regaining functionality. It was about a month before my vision returned to somewhat normal, the ringing in my ears subsided, and my speech started to improve. I could walk around with a cane. But another severe problem had presented itself: My reaction to things were much slower, including my thought processes.

After five long months, I had regained enough functionality to get around on my own, even though I still couldn't feel anything below my knees. At that point the doctors still thought I'd had a stroke, but I felt I needed another opinion. It just didn't add up for me.

I went to see a neurologist. After weeks of testing, CAT scans, and MRIs, he discovered I had multiple sclerosis, or MS. The disease is rare in men, especially men over 60, which I am.

MS is a disease of the central nervous system for which there is no cure. It can affect any part of the body and is progressive, meaning it gets worse over time.

Now that I knew what had caused this traumatic experience in my life, I had to learn how to deal with it. To manage the disease I was given injections of what is referred to as a disease-modifying drug. The drug cost $5,500 per month and does not reverse symptoms but may keep the disease from getting worse.

Working in clients' offices and traveling around town was no longer an option. That changed things for me. I loved marketing and building business websites, but I knew I would have to find a way to serve companies in a way that also fit my physical limitations.

I felt I could take all of the programming and Internet knowledge I had and help others build their skills. I could also build technology-based website programs that would be easy for others to install on their own, without me having to be in the same room.

I started diving into ways to train others on the valuable information I'd gained through my years of website and program development. I also discovered that I could create WordPress plugins to help make their online sales funnels run smoother and even install their own databases for various needs.

This new direction life has taken me has been painful physically, but freeing with my work. It has opened up new opportunities to spread my knowledge in ways I had not thought of before.

Life has a way of throwing curveballs when they're least expected. Getting MS was definitely a curveball I wasn't expecting. I don't wish it on anyone. However, the new path it's taken me down has made me realize just how precious life is and how, even though my body broke, I am not broken. In fact, I'm able to enjoy my life more, while helping others innovate and refine how they do business online.

About the Author

Ron Dowell is from Elizabethtown, Kentucky, and has worked in the computer and Internet industry for over 25 years. He served in the U.S. Air Force at Ellsworth Air Force Base in South Dakota. He has a degree in electronics with an emphasis in computers. He has his MCSE, MCSA, MCP, SCSA, and CompTia A+, Network+, and Security+. He has spent over 20 years as a Web designer and programmer for Fortune 500 companies. Due to a devastating disease that has limited his mobility, he has recently begun creating products and marketing them through JVZoo.

Connect with Ron at:

RonDowell.com
Facebook: facebook.com/ron.dowell.webdesign
Twitter: @ronwebdesign
LinkedIn: linkedin.com/in/ronalddowell

Ron Created:

Funnel Guardian is a complete report on how to protect your sales funnel. It covers everything you need to know and recommends resources. I explain why you need to protect your

sales funnels and discuss how to do it. I recommend several ways to accomplish this, and I even explain how to determine what part of the system is down and the steps to correct the issue. You spent a lot of time building your funnels. Why not make sure they are working as intended?

Find out more at: <u>funnelguardian.com/</u>

Create It Once...Sell it a Million Times

by Marc & Lisa Sylvester

I remember being nine years old, drawing cartoons on ceramic mugs. I bought the special paints and the clay mugs from a local ceramics shop and drew (what I hoped) were funny images of firefighters on them, like fire fighting slogans and images of cats in trees. My parents took me back to the ceramics shop to have the mugs fired in the kiln. When they were done, I took the cartoon mugs to the fire station down the street to sell them to the firefighters for $5 a cup...and they bought them!

Looking back, I think the firemen probably felt sorry for me. My nine-year-old cartoon drawings probably weren't all that great, but I learned early on the concept of creating things to sell—things other people needed or just had to have. Everybody drinks coffee—or at least everybody who worked at the fire station drank coffee, and they all needed firefighting-themed mugs to drink from. Target marketing learned early!

My wife, Lisa, and I own a small Internet business called Laughingbird Software. We've been online since 1995. Lisa works out all of the contracts, financials, and support systems. I work on the graphics, technology, and marketing.

When we were first dating, Lisa was working to get her PhD in psychology. After five years of graduate school, she needed "postdoc hours"—basically 1,500 hours of work under her belt in order to be eligible for licensure. In California, they wanted her to work those 1,500 hours for free.

At the time, I was working at a small business creating graphics. We couldn't make ends meet if she was going to work all those hours with no income! We began looking around the country for an actual paying position. Lucky us, she found a position in Iowa that was right up her alley, so we moved to a really small town.

Lisa began working…and I had nothing to do.

This was back in the day of dial up modems, just as the Internet was starting to take off. It was before the dot-com craze, before YouTube, before cell phones! I began looking closely at this Internet thing, and after a very short while, I knew it was the only way to make a living. With the Internet, I discovered you could create something once and sell it a thousand times. It was the beginning of a beautiful relationship.

While studying the Internet back in the early days, I noticed a lot of mom-and-pop websites popping up all over the place. Daily! These small websites were probably run by people just like me, people sitting in their garages or bedrooms. I figured anybody who worked on the Internet must have their own website, and these people needed images for their sites. I was good at creating images. Cartoons on mugs…why not graphics on websites?

I began creating logos and page header graphics for small businesses on the Net. I created a small niche for myself and was becoming an expert at Web graphics. It was target marketing again. These folks didn't need print graphics. They wanted banners and animated GIF logos. I devoted my time to creating graphics for online use, and it worked out beautifully. I was so busy I couldn't keep up.

There was a problem, though: Customers began asking for alterations— free alterations! This was fine, but it became overwhelming. I thought there must be some way to automate all of it. I did a little research and eventually purchased a software product called Macromedia Director, a programming tool that let you create small software products and games, as well as add graphics or sound to presentations.

I decided to create a tool that would allow customers to create their own logos by dragging images (such as orbs, swooshes, cartoon characters, and the like) onto a canvas and adding text in different fonts. I stopped making graphics for customers and began to program instead.

A year later, after moving back to California and finding ourselves with a beautiful three-year-old daughter and twin baby boys (and after maxing out our credit cards for lack of income!), The Logo Creator was born, and it was a hit!

Lisa and I sold our first version of The Logo Creator for $99. Then we sold it again. And then again! Build it once and sell it a thousand times. It was awesome. As far as I know, The Logo Creator was the very first logo-making tool on the Net.

I couldn't imagine going back to the daily grind of making (and re-making) logos for clients, and Lisa was having so much fun working at home and being with our children that she had no interest in going back to work in her field. We both knew that creating software was the way to go, no ifs, ands, or buts about it. We loved having our own business and working for ourselves rather than for others. And the income potential was unlimited. The harder we worked, the more we made, and the profit was 100% ours, not our employer's.

The hard part about creating software is marketing it. As of this writing, there are probably hundreds of online software programs that will help you create logos, so we needed to stand out from the crowd.

I began learning from crazy Internet gurus like Scott Walker, Andy Jenkins, and Frank Kern—the biggies. After watching the first VideoBoss presentation by Andy Jenkins (and buying the course for a whopping $3K!), I sat back in my chair and thought, "How the heck did he do that?" He pulled all of my emotional triggers and got me to buy a $3,000 course. (By the way, it's a brilliant course and well worth the money a thousand times over.)

I was intrigued, and I spent the next year studying these guys and how they did what they did. I learned that they would collect something called "affiliates"—other people who sold their products for them!

I looked all over the Web for things like "What are affiliates?" and "How to get affiliates," but what I found was confusing and generic. I tried a few different companies that claimed to gather affiliates but the interface and the method of contacting affiliates was ridiculous. It was way too confusing. Just trying to upload a product was incredibly difficult.

Then I happened upon a company called JVZoo. I did a little research and discovered that

a) it was free to use, and

b) it was <u>easy</u> to use! I jumped on it. The interface was really flexible, I could easily link my PayPal account, and they had an incredible built-in network of affiliates, other people looking to sell cool products! In short, it was awesome!

One night, a PayPal alert popped up on my iPad, telling me I'd made $37. I smiled and hit the little 'x' button to close the alert. Seconds later, another PayPal alert popped up. Before I could hit the 'x' button again, another alert popped up. Suddenly my iPad went nuts with alerts and dings! Where the heck were these sales coming from all of a sudden?

The Logo Creator was Product of the Day on JVZoo. It was crazy. The iPad didn't stop buzzing and dinging for two days. The Logo Creator has since been Product of the Day four times! It's a terrific feeling, I'll tell you.

I now only use JVZoo for all of my reselling. There's simply nothing else like it. Lisa and I are not saying this just because we happen to be in a book about JVZoo; we're saying this because it's true and it's awesome.

Build it once, and sell it a thousand times. And then have 100 others sell it 1,000 times. It's a win-win for everyone.

About the Authors

Hi, my name is Marc Sylvester. My wife, Lisa, and I own and run Laughingbird Software. Lisa and I have been running the company since 2001, while living in southern California with our three amazing kids. All three of them have started working with Internet marketing and JVZoo.

Laughingbird Software specializes in graphics. We have software that will help you create logos, banners, marketing graphics, YouTube thumbnails, blog images, even podcast graphics! We have software for Macs, Windows, smart phones, and tablets.

Connect with Marc & Lisa at:

Facebook: <u>facebook.com/Laughingbird.Software</u>

Twitter: @lbsoftware

LinkedIn: <u>linkedin.com/in/marcsylvester</u>

Marc & Lisa Created:

The Logo Creator began as a logo design tool. Over the years, it's grown to be so much more! With The Logo Creator, you'll be able to create amazing marketing graphics like page headers, banners, blog images, YouTube channel art, podcast cover images, Facebook ads, and more! The software comes in Mac, Windows, smart phone, and tablet flavors.

You can use The Logo Creator even if you have very little design skill. It's template-based, and we've created some really cool tutorials to get you up and running quickly. It's fun and easy to use!

Find The Logo Creator at: TheLogoCreator.com

Become A Local Business Marketing Expert

by Andres Tobar

My start in marketing came when I was a sophomore at the University of Florida. I was in school with a focus on premed. I thought that's what I wanted to do, but after two years I was bored. I realized I didn't really want to take the normal path and end up working for someone else.

You see, as far back as I can remember, my father worked for himself. When we lived in Colombia, he owned a rug and upholstery cleaning business servicing residential clients. I remember being eight years old, "helping" him wash rugs on our back patio on the weekends. After we moved to the U.S., he opened a janitorial cleaning business, where I also worked during my high school years. Growing up I never had a real boss and always knew my father as a business owner and manager. It felt natural to follow in his footsteps.

Back to my sophomore year at UF. My father approached me and said he wanted to open a residential carpet cleaning business. He wanted to know what I thought. I said I thought it was a great idea and left it at that. A few weeks later he showed up at our house with a huge carpet cleaning truck, handed me the keys, and said, "Here you go. This is your business, now figure out how to get clients." I hadn't realize when he said that "he" wanted to open a business, it really meant I was going to be in charge of it!

By that time I had mostly stopped going to classes and focused instead on managing the janitorial accounts I was in charge of, so I figured I had plenty of time to start this new business. Along with the keys to the truck, my father also gave me a few binders from a marketing conference for carpet cleaners he had just attended. It was my first introduction to marketing.

The binders were full of strategies and concepts on how to market a carpet cleaning business. I started learning about three step mailings, getting into the mind of the customer, how to write an offer—all the basics of marketing. I also started reading and listening to all the marketing and mindset books I could get my hands on. I mention this because I truly believe that spending all that time absorbing marketing knowledge helped me when I later transitioned from owning a business to being a consultant. But I'll touch on that later.

I decided I wasn't just going to rely on traditional marketing. I would also focus on generating clients online. This was back in 2006 and 2007, so it was not yet common for carpet cleaners to think they could generate clients from the Web. Most were focused on the Yellow Pages and traditional advertising.

Knowing nothing about websites, we hired a web design firm to get our first site up and going. I knew just having a website wouldn't be enough, however, so I learned how to get it to rank in Google. I intuitively knew I wanted our website at the top when people searched "carpet cleaning" in our city. Later on I would come to know that I was learning SEO, or Search Engine Optimization.

My father thought I was a bit crazy for focusing so much time on the website instead of going out and getting our name out there. But back then getting a website to rank was not very difficult, and within a few weeks we were number one in Yahoo and a few weeks later number one in Google. We then started to get a steady stream of customers and quickly filled up our schedule with clients who had found us through the Internet. As our business grew, we were able to invest in other forms of marketing, but no matter what we did, the Internet was still our number one lead generator.

After about a year of running the business, my wife and I had our first son, Nicolas. Little by little I began to realize that maybe this was not what I wanted to do for the rest of my life. I enjoyed the thrill of having a business and being in full control of how much money I made, plus I enjoyed the marketing side of it, but I realized that I did not have a "business." I had a job. I didn't have the freedom to take days off. If I did, I wouldn't bring home any money that day. What's more, I was physically exhausted after a full day of labor and wasn't as playful with my son as I wanted to be.

But I didn't think I knew anything else other than cleaning, since that's what I had been doing all my life. I figured I was stuck and my only option was to grow the business enough to hire employees and get off the truck.

But that changed one day when I was attending another marketing conference for carpet cleaners. The speaker tried to discuss online marketing, but it was such a new topic for the industry that the instructor himself did not have much knowledge on how it could be applied to a typical carpet cleaning business. During the session break I asked the instructor if I could speak for 15 minutes and give other attendees some tips, since we were generating about 90 percent of our clients from the Web. The schedule was so tight they couldn't fit me in, but they did schedule me to come back about a month later to give a one-hour presentation.

I had never given a presentation like this before, so I was a bit nervous, but I figured I knew what I was talking about and I was doing it with the intention of helping fellow business owners. During my talk I explained everything we had done, step by step. I did it in such a way that they could take the information home and start applying it right away.

After finishing the presentation, five or six other business owners asked to contact me to do this for them. I hadn't anticipated that—I mean, I was a carpet cleaner, and I thought that's all I knew how to do. I wasn't a "consultant" or a "marketer." I was just doing this presentation to provide tips and help out. But I quickly realized I had something to offer that they badly needed, and I did not hesitate to seize the opportunity.

I think we often fail to recognize that we all are experts in something, but we don't take advantage of that expertise. If I had not given that one hour talk and those business owners hadn't inquired about my "services," I would probably still be cleaning carpets today.

After the talk that day I began working with a few of those businesses one-on-one, developing their Web strategy. The company that invited me to give the initial presentation liked the first one so much that they started flying me around the country to present full-day workshops in their various locations. Every time I got in front of an audience, I would get five to ten new clients. After doing that for about a year, I was able to grow my consulting business to about 40 monthly on-going clients.

That income gave me the freedom to walk away from the carpet cleaning business and work from home while helping other business owners grow their companies with the power of the Web. After years of doing that, I've now transitioned into building tools and processes that other local business consultants can use to help their clients achieve the same results I did for my clients.

About the Author

Andres Tobar was born in Colombia, South America, and moved the U.S. when he was ten years old. After attending the University of Florida for two years, he decided that it just wasn't for him and started a carpet cleaning business. Within three years it grew to be one of the best companies in Gainesville, Florida. He used what he learned from marketing his company online to start a consulting business helping other small businesses throughout the country. Andres now live in Saint Augustine, Florida, with his wife and their five kids. He develops tools and processes that help other consultants generate leads for their clients.

Connect with Andres at:

AndresTobar.com

Facebook: facebook.com/andresthewebguy

Andres Created:

SERP Shaker is a WordPress plugin that allows the user to build massive sites that target tens of thousands of cities and in turn rank for the long tail in each of those cities. It can be used to promote affiliate offers or create lead-generating sites that you can then sell to local businesses or keep for yourself. You can find it at http://serpshaker.com.

How We Met Bob

by Soren Jordansen

My Best (Imaginary) Friend, Bob

'm Soren Jordansen, co-owner of IM Wealth Builders Ltd., together with my business partners, John Merrick and Cindy Battye. I've been involved with Internet marketing since 2004, and together with my partners have had multiple #1 launches on Clickbank, JVZoo, and our own platforms.

Now, I have limited space for this chapter, and I really want to give you some great advice you can use in your own business, so I'll skip the whole tooting-my-own-horn stuff. After all, there's enough chest-beating in Internet marketing as it is. I want to get right to the juicy stuff. In order for that to happen, I'll introduce you to my good friend, Bob. But first we have to take a quick look at how we met Bob.

From Generation X To Baby Boomers

When we started selling our products on JVZoo, we put the first few up as Warrior Special Offers (WSO) on the Warrior Forum. Each WSO had an embedded sales video hosted on YouTube. After we moved back to self-hosting all of our sales letters, we continued using YouTube videos, even though there are loads of sexier solutions out there—heck, we own a few ourselves.

The reason behind this madness? Google has a (not often talked about) goal of knowing everything about everyone. This is how they are able to serve up relevant search results and ads better than anyone else. It also means that we as marketers can get some really fascinating and useful data about our audience, and one of the ways to collect this data is through YouTube's built-in analytics program.

We have been in this game since 2004, and we have seen a lot of shifts in the marketplace and a lot of trends that have come and gone. Before we started using JVZoo as our main platform, we were selling most of our products on Clickbank. (It was the go-to place five years ago.) We had decent analytics data back then, too, but there was nothing revolutionary in the numbers. Our customers were evenly split between male and female. It was generally a younger crowd—most were in their 20s and 30s, which made perfect sense since all our products related to starting up or running your own Internet business (either as an affiliate or a product vendor).

Fast forward five years. What I noticed when I looked at the analytics data for all our JVZoo sales videos blew my mind!

- 75% of our customers were male!
- 50% of our customers were over 55 years old, with a whopping 88% over 45 years old
- Almost nobody under the age of 34

In other words, we had gone from selling to Generation X to marketing to the Baby Boomers.

After wracking my brain trying to figure out why we had seen such a massive shift in our audience, the proverbial penny finally dropped…The change in demographics was due to the financial crisis that shook the world in 2008 and is still sending ripples through society.

Many people lost their jobs or saw their 401(k)s, pensions, and life savings disappear into thin air. The lucky ones who kept their jobs and savings still came out increasingly worried about their financial future. This created a new demand in the Internet marketing industry, with older people joining the ranks, trying to start online businesses in hopes of replacing their lost income or savings, or to create a greater personal buffer against the machinations of the "one percent."

With this in mind, the shift in gender composition is relatively easy to explain as well. Like it or not, in most families all over the world, the man is still the main breadwinner, so in the wake of the crisis more men sought our products in order to maintain that role. It's not that the women stopped buying our products, and neither did younger people—the influx of middle aged and older men was just big enough to shift the average considerably.

The first place we noticed this shift was in our support desk. We were getting an unusual number of support tickets, and they were asking technical questions that we had never imagined anyone would ask. But it's quite obvious when you think about it: Your average 25-year-old is more tech savvy than your average 65-year-old.

Of course there are exceptions, but where previously we could just ask people to FTP something to their site, the same instructions now create a slew of tickets asking how to do that. It's not a major problem; we quickly adjusted and started making our tutorial videos more step-by-step, more beginner-friendly, and much more detailed.

It didn't completely fix the problem, though. You can have the best tutorials in the world, but it won't matter if nobody watches them. We also used YouTube for hosting our tutorials, and the analytics told us that 60 percent of the tutorial video views were from women. As you'll recall, women only made up 25 percent of our customer base. These stats thus reinforced the old stereotype of men not reading manuals or asking for directions.

In order to combat this we had to develop a whole new way of delivering our training. Previously we would have all our tutorials for a product on a separate page and with just a few long videos. We revamped all of our products, including a step-by-step set-up process, with the tutorial videos inside the product and with much shorter bite-sized videos. It was a success! Men may not seek out the tutorials, but if you put them in front of them in short 30-second bits, odds are they will watch. Doing this significantly decreased the number of support tickets.

Now, this was all about reacting to a change in our demographics and adjusting our existing products. Armed with the data, we were proactive and developed our new products with the new target market in mind. And to do that, we wanted to get a better grip on to whom exactly we were selling.

Meet Bob

Armed with our analytics and U.S. census data, plus equal parts imagination and intuition, my good friend, Simon Hodgkinson, and I sat down to write up a description of our average customer.

His name is Bob and he is likely to live (or want to live) in Florida. He is a white, middle aged to retirement level male—disgruntled with working for a living, worried his job will disappear, concerned his pension won't last, and looking to create a secondary income stream or a replacement for his current one.

Bob is probably not looking to build an online empire (too old and jaded), but is doing this perhaps for some extra retirement money and something to pass on to the kids down the road.

He looks at your lifestyle and wants it, but would moderate the excesses, as his church wouldn't approve. Bob is likely to lean to the right (moderate conservative at minimum), and he regrets not having the guts to walk away from the rat race earlier in life. Right now he probably earns around $40-50K per year in a white-collar role, likely to be services based. He probably has two kids in their mid to late teens and a ton of debt (house, car, furniture, credit cards, etc.)

This is the avatar for our customers. When I develop ideas for new products, write promotional emails, or write sales letters, I do it for Bob! I can't stress enough how much easier it becomes when you flesh out your target market like this. Lots of trial and error can be eliminated by asking yourself simple questions like, "Would Bob buy this?" or "Would Bob approve of this message?"

Your average customer avatar may be very different from Bob. She might be a 30-year-old woman interested in vegan recipes. But if you are selling JVZoo products either as an affiliate or a vendor, chances are Bob will work for you, too. Because of the way JVZoo works, with the "Product of the Day" mailings and vendors promoting each other's products, the customer lists have a lot of overlap, and odds are your data is very similar to ours.

We have tried ignoring Bob and created a product that really wasn't for him. As you can imagine, the result was nothing to brag about.

We designed a very clever WordPress theme called Covert Viral Wizard. In my opinion, it's one of our best and most useful products. It's based on Tumblr, though, both mimicking it and using it for viral traffic generation. Now, as you may know, Tumblr is extremely popular with young people (ages 15 to 30). Bob, on the other hand, couldn't care less about Tumblr and probably doesn't even know what it is.

The end result was that we did not sell as many copies as we would have liked, and we had to spend a lot of effort selling the virtues of Tumblr, rather than what our theme can accomplish with it.

On the other hand, take our best-selling theme, Covert Store Builder. It is an Amazon-based affiliate store theme. We were cooking with gas on this one, because Bob knows Amazon, he shops on Amazon, and so do his wife and kids. We did not have to sell Bob on the idea of Amazon; he immediately got it and wanted our theme so he could carve himself a slice of the pie.

End result: Covert Store Builder went on to break multiple sales records on JVZoo and was the most-sold product in the marketplace for over a year. Do <u>not</u> ignore Bob!

I hope you have enjoyed these insights into our customer demographics and how we use that data. To recap, here are the steps I highly recommend you implement in your business today:

- Use Google Analytics, YouTube Analytics, and similar to get all the data you can on your customers—then figure out the average numbers.
- Use national statistics, census data, etc. to flesh out your average number.
- Write up a bio for your avatar—your average customer—and create your own "Bob."
- Go through your existing email series, products, etc. and make sure they resonate with your avatar.
- When you create new products, write emails, write sales letters, etc., <u>always</u> do so specifically for your customer avatar.

It doesn't matter if you market JVZoo products as an affiliate or sell your own products. If you follow these steps, I guarantee you will see an increase in your conversions and sales!

P.S. If you happen to fit my description of Bob and you are one of our customers, I owe you a fine bottle of Scotch, since you have made us quite a bit of money. Thank you, Bob!

About the Author

One-third of the IM Wealth Builders team, Soren Jordansen is a Danish citizen living in Belgrade, Serbia, with his wife and new baby boy. Soren is a former officer in the Danish army, who started his Internet marketing career in 2004. He began as an affiliate, but shortly after he started developing his own products and membership sites. He quit his job in the army in mid-2006 to focus entirely on his Internet marketing business; as he says, "Writing copy is a lot safer than getting shot at!" Soren is the company wordsmith, in charge of copywriting, email marketing, and product ideas (that is, coming up with a billion weird ideas to annoy the other two owners).

Connect with Soren at:

IMWealthBuilders.com

Facebook: facebook.com/pages/IM-Wealth-Builders/293241964070001

Twitter: @SorenJordansen

LinkedIn: linkedin.com/company/im-wealth-builders-ltd-/

Soren Co-Created:

Join the elite ranks at the Covert Commission HQ to discover the top secret and shockingly simple turnkey system for banking massive affiliate checks without a website or product of your own.

Find out more at: covertcommissionhq.com

My Journey From $120k in DEBT to building a 7-Figure Business

by Ankur Shukla

ost successful entrepreneurs will only tell you about their successes. That's usually just the tip of the iceberg, though. Those massive successes and achievements are only a small percentage of the entire story. The rest (that they're not sharing) contains the most valuable lessons. As Mr. Bill Gates said, "It's fine to celebrate success but it is more important to heed the lessons of failure." I hope my story will motivate you and teach you some very valuable lessons.

When I moved to Bangalore in 2012, I found myself in a very difficult situation. I was 28 years old, newly wed, and without a job. I had absolutely no source of income. On top of that, I was also $120,000 in debt! Banks wanted nothing to do with me. My savings were completely gone. Things were not looking good.

How could I have gotten myself in this deep dark hole? How could I let all this happen to me? Let's rewind a bit to see how I got into this mess in the first place...and how you can avoid getting into the same dark situation.

In 2010, I had a cushy, high-paying job at a new, fast-growing e-learning company. It doubled in size every few months. Every year we moved into a bigger office. I worked very hard during this time, and I helped the company grow 400 percent in less than two years.

My Dream Led to Disaster

I had always dreamt of owning a big house, and I wanted to buy one for my parents, too. When the right opportunity came along, I put almost all my savings into buying a home, with almost 50 percent to be paid in parts over the next four years—hence the $120k debt. I thought I had meticulously calculated everything. I felt confident that I'd do well over the next few years to pay it all off, without the need for a bank loan.

Things didn't pan out quite as I had hoped. A few months after investing in this "dream," the unexpected happened. To my surprise, the company I was working for started to run out of cash! It was devastating to me, as I had invested a lot of my own time (and money) into this company. I had hired and built a team of over 50 people. And when the company started to run out of cash, they gave me the gut-wrenching assignment to let go of half of these 50 dedicated employees. It was one of the worst experiences of my life. Little did I know, however, that all of these difficulties would become a blessing in disguise.

No Such Thing as a Secure Job

Telling all those people they no longer had a job made me realize that there's no such thing as a secure job. You can lose your job at any moment. This was a truly eye-opening revelation for me. It made me more interested in the idea of working for myself, and it made me realize I was actually an entrepreneur at heart.

When I looked back, I realized I had been an entrepreneur my entire life. I started my first comic book business at the age of 14. After turning that into a profitable venture, I was hooked. I built other tiny businesses while I was at school. At age 18, I started a small ad agency that made over 60 TV commercials for the local station. At age 20, I sold payroll software for a pretty penny. I started to notice a pattern—entrepreneurship was and always had been in my blood!

Taking The Plunge as an Entrepreneur

As soon as I realized I wanted nothing to do with a job, I got to work! I went to online forums and learned again how to build websites and SEO, but most importantly, I started from scratch and taught myself <u>a lot</u> about Internet marketing.

A good friend always said that when starting something new, it is best to start from a position of advantage. So I started with what had worked really well for me when I was in college. I had stumbled upon Joel Comm's <u>The AdSense Code</u> and was very successful with building niche websites and generating revenue with Google AdSense. This strategy was no longer as good as it was back in 2006 (ah, the golden days), but it still worked very well.

While working to build more passive income online, I found myself spending time in many online forums, especially Warrior Forum. I saw a small handful of people creating and selling products and making a lot of money, so I figured I'd give it a shot.

Taking Action: My First Ever Product Launch

In early 2013, I decided to create and sell my very first product online. Massive success, right? Wrong. It was a huge flop. I spent almost two weeks creating it. I made sure it was unique. And a lot of my peers told me it would sell really well. Nope. It only made 15 sales during its first week after launch.

Looking back, I did a lot of things wrong with this one—bad sales copy, poor positioning of the product, lack of testimonials, not enough global appeal, not enough proof to back up my claims, and so on. But I tried to not let this flop beat me up. I wanted to keep going. I wanted to do better on the next one.

The Strategy That Worked

I decided to reach out to some bigger names in the online marketing community to ask for their feedback on why my product didn't sell well. Most people ignored my messages, but a few gave me really valuable insight.

Here's the kicker: Reaching out to people, asking them for feedback and advice, was exactly how I found my first launch partner—someone who'd already had great success with previous launches and who already had a list of loyal customers who might buy my product. All we had to do was tweak the positioning of my product and improve the sales funnel a bit.

We re-launched it on JVZoo.com. On the first day, we made over 600 sales, bringing in over $10,000 in revenue and winning Product of the Day on JVZoo! We closed the week with over 1,400 units sold and over $25,000 in revenue from the launch. I was ecstatic!

And here are some of my biggest takeaways:

- Great product + great sales copy = Great launch. :)
- It is okay to not know everything. Find people who do.
- If your product sells well, it will attract affiliates like a magnet.
- Build great relationships with your affiliates and treat them well. Think long term!
- Never stop networking.
- The money is in the list. Focus on building a big buyers list.

I Finally Found My Passion

I soon discovered that I absolutely loved solving problems using technology. This became my passion: to build products that solve a niche problem for a lot of people. For 12 months, I built several products and partnered with more people to launch them. Looking back, all I really did was repeat the process behind the first successful launch I had.

The Simple Four-Step Formula That Works Every Time

It doesn't matter what niche you're in. You'll make a ton of money if you follow this simple proven formula.

- Find a problem.
- Identify a process to solve it.
- Create a training product OR a software product that solves the problem in a faster, easier, and more efficient way.
- Launch it on your own, or find a partner who has done something similar and is well known in that niche and launch it with him or her.

This simple formula catapulted my business.

People are (and always will be) happy to buy products that solve their problems. It doesn't matter if it's information products, video training, or software. Help them solve their problems, and you will be rewarded tenfold.

My Biggest Home Run To Date

Over the course of a year of repeating my four-step formula, I sold over 10,000 copies of digital products online. In August 2014, my business went to a new level. I launched a product that became the #3 top-selling product of all time on JVZoo.com. It sold over 15,000 copies in the first four weeks! It was by far my biggest product launch ever.

That same month, I had the privilege to attend and interview top marketing experts at JVZoo's Marketing Mayhem event in Orlando, Florida. I met hundreds of people and finally got over my fear of public speaking. I even got to shake hands with the guy who inspired my first taste of entrepreneurial success, Mr. Joel Comm himself, and become part of this book. Networking and building new friendships has taken things to a whole new level, and I look forward to shattering my personal records in 2015.

Looking back, I really doubted myself at times. We can be our own worst critic. Today, I am proud to say that I'm 100 percent debt-free and I now run a very profitable business from the comfort of my own home. I enjoy waking up every day to continue to build solutions to people's problems.

I hope my story has inspired you to not give up on your dreams and to work with passion to achieve success. I want to leave you with a few words my good friend and launch partner, Spencer, spoke the other day: "If you focus on your problems, you'll have more problems. If you focus on possibilities, you'll have huge opportunities."

Stay positive. Try not to focus on the problems at hand. Focus instead on what you're capable of and get to work on it. My guess is you're far more capable than you think you are. As long as you build a simple solution that fixes a problem many people have, you'll never have to worry about money again.

About the Author

Ankur Shukla is a digital marketer and product creator from Bangalore, India. He has built over 100 websites and created 15+ digital products selling to over 25,000 customers across the globe. He loves to find problems he can solve using technology and turns them into innovative products. Ankur is also an active member of the startup community in Bangalore, where he likes to meet fellow entrepreneurs and help them with their marketing, while also being an advisor/mentor to a few companies. He loves to cook, live in various parts of the world, ride roller coasters, and adventure in life. You can contact him via his website for free business/online marketing advice.

Connect with Ankur at:

AnkurShukla.com

Facebook: facebook.com/ankur14vicky

Twitter: @ankurshuklacom

LinkedIn: linkedin.com/in/ankurshukla

Ankur Created:

WP Freshstart is a WordPress plugin that lets you setup a WordPress site in under seven seconds. It takes care of optimizing settings in WordPress, creating required legal and disclaimer pages, and deleting anything that typical websites/blogs do not need on the site. This plugin has been installed on over 20,000 websites by more than 7,000 users. You can find this at: http://wpfreshstart.com

Make The Journey Simpler

by Brett Ingram

Maybe it was luck, but I don't believe that. In 2006, I was searching online when I stumbled upon a sales page for some e-book. I didn't want the e-book, but the idea of a product that could be sold and delivered instantly over the Internet got my entrepreneurial gears turning. I thought about the income potential of selling digital products online—low startup cost, minimal overhead, and instant access to a massive customer base—and I started digging to figure out how I could do it myself.

Stumbling on that e-book sales page may have been luck, but the context of my life compelled me to take action and become an Internet marketer. I was a typical guy with a full-time job, a wife and kids, a mortgage and car payments, and I was attending graduate school at night to get my MBA. We were getting by, but I wanted more than that for my family. I wanted to create a lifestyle of wealth and freedom. I had planned on becoming a management consultant and working my way up the ladder—until a simple phone call changed my life.

I was at school on a Wednesday night. I had woken up at 6:00 that morning, dropped my son at daycare, rolled into the office and worked a full day, then took the train into the city to get to my graduate school class. During break between classes at 7:30 pm, I called home, and my wife said she was reading a bedtime story to our son, Brett. I felt empty and sad because I was 65 miles away at school and was missing such a special moment. Even worse, it occurred to me that as a consultant—living out of hotels during the week—I would miss all of the bedtime stories.

I decided that day, regardless of the time and money I had spent pursuing the consulting career I thought I wanted, I would change paths and do something where I had the freedom to make my own schedule. That's what drove me the day I saw that e-book.

I officially started my Internet business in June 2006, but the road was not clear and straight for me. I was alone. I had no mentors, no friends in the business, no extra disposable income to play with, and only a few hours of free time each week to work on my business. It took me months to learn the basics of online marketing because the more I learned, the more stuff I discovered that I didn't know yet. I was trying to take it all in, process it, and make some kind of meaningful plan. It was overwhelming.

Finally I decided to just start. I knew if I just kept learning, I'd be the smartest broke guy in the industry. The only way to actually build an Internet business is to just start doing it. So I did. I set up my first website. Then I created my first e-book. Looking back, they were so bad it makes me laugh now. But the important point was that I was building momentum. I was getting stuff done. I was making progress, and every step was one step closer to my goal.

Then, three months after starting my new venture, disaster struck. I was running late for class and missed the train into the city. I drove my car instead and parked outside under a street light. I was late, and in the rush I forgot my briefcase in the back seat of my car. Once inside, I realized I'd forgotten it but decided to leave it since I parked on a highly-traveled, well-lit street.

When I returned to my car after class, I stared in shock at the smashed rear window and empty back seat where my briefcase had been. It was gone, along with my zip drive that contained all of my marketing knowledge, my data, and my work. My entire business was gone just like that. I couldn't believe it. I searched frantically around the nearby bushes and trash cans, hoping the thief had dumped it when he realized there was no money in it. No luck.

I was furious, completely frustrated, and in despair. I felt like the world was against me and thought about giving up. But after the waves of anger and frustration passed, I focused again on <u>why</u> I was trying to build an online business in the first place, and I refused to quit.

It took me seven months to make my first $17 sale, but after thirteen months I quit my job and was running my business full-time. Once I understood the process for making money online, it was just a matter of scaling it larger and doing it faster. Since my start, I have created and launched over 40 products and websites, generated well into the seven figures in sales, and helped thousands of other entrepreneurs and online marketers.

I create products and services that help online marketers simplify, automate, and accelerate their success. I remember the challenges I had getting started and how different my life would be if I hadn't stuck with it. Despite having no mentors, no friends in the business, and no nest egg to fall back on, I did it. If I can help others—by making the journey simpler—I feel like I can be the difference that helps someone stick with it until they get there, when they might have otherwise quit. That's what drives my business passion.

Just as important, I now have the personal freedom to work from home so I can take part in the things that are important to me.

So what advice would I offer someone who wants to build an Internet business? Three simple things...

1. Follow your passion—the best way to build a successful online business (or any business for that matter) is to do what you love. If you love making pizza, start a business about making pizza. Too many people fall into the trap of trying to chase the money. They see something that's popular and jump into it because they think there is money to be made. The problem with this is, with any business there will be obstacles, and if you don't love what you do it will feel like work and you'll want to quit. When what you do comes from your passion, you have an endless supply of energy to push you through anything that stands in your way.

2. Provide value to your customer. Building a business isn't about making money. It's about providing enough value to your customers that they want to exchange their money for it. When you give awesome value to your customers, they will wait in line to buy what you offer. This is the real business secret, the secret that makes two of the biggest challenges business owners face—competitors and finding new customers—all but disappear.

3. Focus and be decisive. There are so many options when you're building an online business, from the types of products and services you offer to the traffic methods you'll use, and a million things in between. Don't try to be all things to all people. You'll just wind up losing your whole customer base to a bunch of marketers who specialize. They will each take the share of the market they provide for best, leaving you with nothing. Get in the habit of making decisions quickly. Decide what your company stands for, what you offer, and who you serve. Stick to that, and say no to all distractions. You'll be amazed by how fast you can build a successful business when you have clarity.

If there's a lesson in my story, I hope you take from it the courage to follow your dreams. Know that you are not alone, and no matter what challenges you face, you can do it. Never give up. People overcome incredible odds to do amazing things every day, and so can you.

About the Author

 Brett has been a full-time Internet marketer since 2007. He has developed and launched dozens of products that help people make money online, and his products and coaching are responsible for many other marketers' success stories.

He started his online business with no experience, no mentors, a family at home, and while working full-time and attending graduate school. Because he built his business despite these challenges, he knows he can help anyone who is committed to being successful.

Brett has an MBA from New York University with specializations in Strategy, Leadership and Change Management, and Finance.

Connect with Brett at:

Brett-Ingram.com

Facebook: facebook.com/brett.a.ingram

Twitter: @brett_ingram

Brett Created:

The 100K eBiz Formula is a complete step-by-step system for building a $100,000 per year Internet business. It is comprised of eight modules that walk you through every step—from picking a niche, to creating a product, to setting up your website, to driving traffic, and more. The 100K eBiz Formula is based on over seven years of experience and knowledge of what works, and the methods and tactics are proven. You get videos, audios, PDF  downloads, workbooks, and checklists plus one-on-one coaching and software tools to keep you on track and get it done. Fin it at: 100kebizformula.com

Getting To "There": How To Build A Business Model

by Rick Mortimer

W alk with me through the evolution of a spectacular business model. Those who have read my latest book, The 60 Minute MBA, will know the primacy I place on building a business model suited to the entrepreneur, to present a business idea in the most profitable way possible. Here, then, is a condensed summary of the trials and triumphs that have culminated in the creation of my current business vehicle, ChangeAgent Consulting, and its latest product, a complete marketing, selling, and follow-up system for a wide variety of businesses, which we call The Happy Bulldog™. ChangeAgent has become a full-service marketing and management consulting firm, capable of delivering most of the products and services that online or offline businesses need.

My mission for several years has been to develop a business model that supports new entrepreneurs, especially those facing a lack of money as they near or hit retirement age. As often happens, that mission has been achieved by a series of false starts and stumbles, exploratory probes into the infinite possibilities that designing a fresh approach demands.

My method begins with the desired end point and works backward; this forces every element of the business model to be evaluated in reverse, each proving its consistency with the desired final outcome. Start with the requirements and constraints of the entrepreneur. In this case, we are designing for a generalized entrepreneur as well as for myself personally.

My personal income target, once a business has achieved scale after a few years, is a net income of $50,000 per month. This income must be sustainable even as my attention to the business diminishes, resulting in 90 percent hands-off, passive income within five years. If incomes for the entrepreneurs who join me range between 50 and 150 percent of this objective, that will be adequate and consistent with my mission.

Next, we move to constraints and prerequisites. Clearly, I can't design a business that fits everyone. At a minimum, those I invite in must have an extremely strong background in business management, and an equally strong background in Internet technologies, marketing, and communications. These are my strong suits. While this requirement will eliminate many, I can say with certainty that there are tens of thousands of older people who have accumulated vast expertise in all of these areas, through decades of experience in the workforce. I want to focus on these people, the ones I <u>can</u> help.

Individual constraints will vary widely, so we are going to shoot for the characteristics that should include a high percentage of the prospective entrepreneurs. First, the model must support very limited capital availability; it must be bootstrap-friendly. Second, it must accommodate a wide variety of the health, mobility, and energy level limitations that visit most of us as we age. Robustness and flexibility must be built-in characteristics. Recurring income, which can be transitioned to passive recurring income, is essential.

There are six characteristics that I have come to recognize as must-haves for any business model to have great potential, as I detailed in my book. Here, we will give each just the briefest of explanations.

The product or service must present a compelling solution to a great need or problem in the marketplace; a starving market must exist, rather than a marginal demand. The business must be macro-aligned, meaning that it is positioned to ride the largest current long-term waves of societal and economic change, rather than be swamped by them.

Barriers to entry for future competitors must either exist or be constructible. There must be no need for outside investment capital for at least three to five years, so the entrepreneur can make all decisions based on his or her long-term outlook and goals.

There must be a clear pathway to scale, a combination of factors that allow the business to grow to meet the minimum income requirements of the entrepreneur within a short time. And finally, a route to time freedom for the entrepreneur must exist as an inherent element of the model.

With all of these thoughts held front-of-mind, so begins the process of 'ideate and iterate.' This is a lengthy series of thought experiments, starting with one or two of the above requirements, suggesting new combinations for the marketplace, and then testing mentally for the existence of a single model that satisfies all of them. I do it in a dark room, going deep inside my imagination. Others may do best masterminding with like-minded people. Either way, very few initial ideas make it through the many screens.

Ideas that do make it through must be tested in the real world; most of them will contain unforeseen land mines or brick walls that must be discovered with a minimum of time, effort, and pain. With each rejected idea, more information is acquired. Eventually, a model meeting <u>all</u> of the criteria emerges from the debris. The process can be grueling, but it does work, given enough time and persistence.

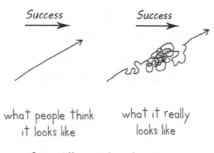

what people think   what it really
it looks like   looks like

from AlligatorSunglasses.com

My current journey has had almost as many twists and turns as the cartoon above, but one common element emerged early in the process and has been a part of every iteration: a core emphasis on Internet technologies. This is not only because it has become central to most people's lives, but because it is both a connector and a transaction engine that allows people with limited mobility or health issues to participate fully in economic growth.

On the scrapheap are experiments with a by-owner real estate marketplace, affiliate marketing, product development in the 'making money online' space, several broad Internet marketing efforts, and even a foray into digital learning products with elements of multilevel marketing.

We must not omit development and control of proprietary products. Those who expect to do well by promoting someone else's product have not yet learned the enormous range of techniques and tricks for diverting sales at the last moment. When you control the product, at least you always control half of the transaction.

Also, the competition among product makers in the Internet marketing space is extremely fierce. The guys who dominate IM have been around for years and have assembled great teams and nearly unlimited capital—not to mention lists and affiliate lists that touch virtually every interested human being on the planet, several times over. To compete in that space is to compete, more directly than is at first obvious, with guys like Mike Filsaime, Frank Kern, Andy Jenkins, Russell Brunson, Dan Kennedy, and Matt Bacak. There are 20 other top-tier names, and another 200 second-tier. That's probably not a good plan.

But from the smoke and steam of the scrapheap, a new vision emerges. It is borne of the realization that another, far larger market exists for those capable of designing and delivering similar products—and this market is underserved and highly fragmented. It is the market for products and services needed by traditional, non-Internet focused businesses worldwide. They have a steady flow of money to spend and a long list of needs, including SEO, PPC, ongoing website tuning, e-commerce, social media presence, reputation management, video marketing, mobile marketing, list capture and management, conversion enhancement…The list is endless.

Quick—name the dominant providers. You may come up with names in a few categories, but you will see that there are gaping holes in coverage. Yet most of these services can be provided, either directly or via outsourcing, by most reasonably experienced Internet marketers.

In addition, there is an overarching need common to all businesses: new tools and techniques to increase revenues. This means more leads, one way or another, with better follow-up systems that convert ever-higher percentages to paying customers.

The fact that the traditional business market is underserved is not intuitively obvious to the casual observer. In fact, first impressions after moving into the market are that it is saturated. Most business owners will tell you, without exaggeration, that they are cold-approached (phone, email, walk-in) by people hawking some "Internet something," over 20 times per week.

Yet the market <u>is</u> underserved—it is just <u>over-pitched</u> by salespeople with one product to sell and one approach in their pitch book. Many business owners have given up trying to differentiate between Internet services and are very quick to pull the "go away" trigger. They are aware that they have many unfilled needs, but they are fully occupied by running their businesses in the day-to-day, and they have an abundance of mistrust for "Internet something" salespeople. We have found that if we can break through the initial resistance, and over-deliver on a small, inexpensive initial service, the floodgates open. Once trust is established, their many needs come pouring out, and at ChangeAgent.co, we have built the capacity to satisfy most of them.

Our point of entry is their universal and perpetual need for increased revenues. It is far easier to get an owner talking about increasing his or her cash flow than anything else we have found. Our leadoff service can be derived from one small element of our Happy Bulldog™ marketing, selling, and follow-up system.

Just as often, the resulting conversation with the owner will lead us in a whole different direction, because above all, we want to follow their pain, however it may be presented to us. We guide them in this crucial first conversation to expound on their toughest problems, thus amplifying their pain—in their own words, spoken to us, rather than by us. Then we simply propose a solution. This solution does not have to be all-encompassing or complete—in fact it should not be—just a step in the right direction. Simple. Cheap. Easily deliverable, quickly.

This transaction sets the stage for great and wonderful things to follow. No matter the size of the project or product, if we over-deliver on all of our initial promises to the business owner and show the capacity to do much more, we have a client for life. Continuing to under-promise and over-deliver is the easy part. Getting into that critical first conversation is the key!

About the Author

Rick Mortimer is a grizzled veteran of bootstrap startups. He executed his first in 1968, at the age of 16, hiring high school and college students as independent contractors to perform odd jobs for homeowners.

He went on to secure a degree in Biology from Lafayette College (a great school, but not particularly relevant to SBOs). His first million dollar (revenues) company was North American Tool Corp., founded in 1979. His first Internet operation was Illuma.net, started in 1994 as an independent ISP—a spectacular, venture-funded failure.

Several great successes later, his primary vehicle today is ChangeAgent.co, a full-service marketing consulting firm, with forces spread across the globe, from Cebu City in the Philippines to Palm Coast, Florida, where he resides.

He is the author of The 60 Minute MBA and a co-author of Playday to Payday.

He can be reached at rm@ChangeAgent.co, or by calling the Florida office at (866) 468-9086.

My Escape From Chemical Suicide

by Dan Brown

I may not have met you, but I think I know a little about you. You've realized that some people are making tons of money online and that many others are making a good living without dragging themselves to a J.O.B. (Just Over Broke) every day.

That's why you're reading this book, isn't it?

Maybe you've tried it yourself but didn't make the kind of money you needed to set yourself free. Or maybe you haven't tried at all because you just don't know how.

I don't know exactly where you are in your life, what kind of job you have, or how much money you're bringing in, but before I go any further, I'd like to tell you a little about who I am and what I do. Like why the heck should you read this anyway?

My name is Dan Brown. I've spent my entire professional career in Internet marketing, and I've been fortunate enough to have some pretty impressive results over the years. I'm not telling you this to brag, but to show you what the right strategies and the right knowledge can do for your bank account (and your lifestyle).

Of all the strategies I use, list building is the single most important. Heavy hitters like David Ogilvy, Frank Kern, Dan Kennedy, and Gary Halbert all built their empires on lists. Now, my techniques (just like these guys') aren't what the "gurus" teach.

I'll tell you about it shortly, but don't think for a minute that I was always an expert. I used to be just like you. When I first started I had so many problems keeping me up at night, watching the paint peel. I suffered from serious stagnation.

Do you struggle because you don't know where to start or what to do? Do you spend hours tirelessly trying to grow your online business, only to be disappointed by low sales every month? Are you frustrated with low conversions, bad lead quality, and a business that just won't grow?

I was overwhelmed big time that first year. I was in way over my head. My lack of success was glaringly obvious. In fact, many times I felt like I was actually moving backward...no sales, no commissions, and no clicks to show for my efforts, just a maxed out credit card and dwindling bank account.

I've been there and experienced every single one of these failures time and time again. But I'm thankful I didn't quit, because things are much different now. Let me tell you a true story.

My Escape From Chemical Suicide

Have you ever been inside a real chemical plant? Nothing you've seen on TV or in the movies can prepare you for the shock of being inside a real chemical processing plant. The sounds, the smell, the sight of all those harmful chemicals spilling out of the deteriorating barrels is completely devastating to one's health.

You can feel your skin start to tingle as soon as you walk through the front doors. It reeks of artificial death, and before long you are convinced that your lungs are shredding to pieces from the toxic fumes penetrating your heavy suit. There are simply no words to convey precisely what being inside a place like this is like. I know because I almost spent my whole life trapped inside one.

You see, this was long before I started pulling down thousand dollar days using a complete auto-pilot system of list building that I am about to share with you. This was back when I was working for pennies doing the bottom-rung work. I would come home every night from that awful job just exhausted and sick from all the fumes I was inhaling. My coworkers were leaving left and right because the work was too hard and too dangerous for any human to do for longer than a few short months.

If it weren't for the long, hard struggle I went through learning how to build solid, revenue-generating businesses on command, I would either be dead from the toxic fumes I was inhaling or homeless because I would have had to quit my only job.

I am not telling you this so you feel sorry for me. The opposite is true. I am telling you this because I want you to fully understand how powerful this system is that I am about to share with you...right here in this chapter 100% free!

Digital marketing saved my life! I know it sounds cliché, but it's completely true. I was able to completely ditch the job scene that almost took my life.

If this whole online business thing can work for me, it can certainly work for you! But it's not easy (and even nearly impossible without the right tools). I used to spend tons of money buying "fool-proof" e-books, video courses, seminars, and anything else I could get my hands on, with nothing to show for my investment. I stumbled around on my own, determined to create my own "perfect method" for generating sales.

I lost trust in the gurus who promised the silver bullet. I suffered through month after month of no results and no progress toward freeing myself from the daily grind. I wasted countless hours chasing push button methods, time that I know now is lost forever!

I was so frustrated from wasting time and money, from trusting the gurus who made promises but were obviously keeping the real secrets of success to themselves, that I decided right then and there that when I finally found the answers, I would share them with other hard-working entrepreneurs without holding back.

Because I've been where you are, and I firmly believe that a dog and pony show isn't an ethical way to do business. Hard-working people deserve real, practical solutions, not flimsy theories that just don't work in the real world!

Fortunately, the solution was right under my nose all along! Some people call it luck. Others call it serendipity. Whatever you want to call it, it was a moment that changed my life forever. One day, when I wasn't even thinking about my business struggles, it hit me. I suddenly realized why every single one of the methods I had tried had failed.

Honestly, I don't know where it came from, but it was like finally breathing air after being held underwater for what seemed like eternity! This incredible moment of clarity seemed almost too good to be true. Even though I secretly doubted my epiphany, I went to work.

Incredibly enough, that moment of clarity transformed me from an exhausted chemical recycler into a digital marketing expert. Even more amazingly, I became the go-to guy for others wanting to build their lists and grow their profits! People even started asking me to teach them everything I knew (which is a great feeling, I have to admit).

I remembered the promise I made to myself when I was struggling with making money online. I couldn't keep it all to myself. I owed it to talented, hard-working people like you to cut through the noise and reveal the true techniques for building a lifestyle business without holding back! With this model you can get started pulling in solid income so reliable you can set your watch to the deposits hitting your account each and every day!

If you want to make at least six figures online this year I'm going to show you how right now. All you need is to focus on three things:

1. Create a landing page so you can build a subscriber list
2. Get traffic
3. Get conversions

That's it! Seems easy enough, right? Well, it is! This is the same business model that companies have been using for many years:

1. Give away something awesome for free.
2. Get a bunch of people who want that free giveaway and trade that freebie for their contact information.
3. Sell them something down the road now that you have their contact info. (This can even be automated!)

It is one of the simplest ways to guaranteed profits! It's going to be even simpler for you, because if you let me, I will hand you your own Internet business based on this model. If you stick around, I'll give you the exact step-by-step process to turn the next 30 days into the last 30 days of your J.O.B., so you can make a six-figure income with your business.

There is a plug-n-play process for attaining this success system, one so powerful that today you can begin seeing a reliable and predicable income source come to life right before your very eyes. And most importantly, this can be yours less than 24 hours from now!

Click the link in my bio and join me inside the Green Room so we can get started!

About the Author

Dan Brown is the go-to entrepreneur on digital and Internet marketing success in the new economy. His fast-moving videos and seminars on digital marketing, list building, email marketing, affiliate marketing, and overall business strategy are loaded with powerful, proven ideas and strategies that people can immediately apply to get better results and live a more ideal lifestyle.

As my way of saying thanks for reading about me in The Rockstars of JVZoo, I've put together a special offer for you to join The Green Room risk free and enjoy the ultimate guide to digital marketing success. I strive to give you the most cutting-edge and ground-breaking content I possibly can because my goal with this club is to cover everything from A to Z so you can build a consistent and reliable lifestyle business! Get the Ultimate Guide to Digital Marketing Success here: DanBrown.tv/rockstars.

Connect with Dan on:
DigitalMarketingHive.com
Facebook: facebook.com/DanBrownTV
Twitter: @TheNewDanBrown
LinkedIn: ca.linkedin.com/in/danieljoshuabrown

The Importance Of Passive Income

by David Perdew

Will You Be Prepared When Your Life Changes In Ways You Didn't Expect?

My phone vibrated in my hand, and I knew immediately it was trouble. I washed down a mouthful of cinnamon roll with some hot coffee at the University of Alabama homecoming tent, and I answered my sister's call while my heart rose in my chest.

It was a beautiful, crisp Saturday morning, perfect for a college football game. People were celebrating all around us, waving banners and clinking red plastic cups filled with mimosas. But getting a call from my sister on that morning sucked all the sunshine out of the sky.

I had plenty of reasons to be nervous. My 85-year-old dad had been in rehab for two months recovering from his right hip replacement surgery on September 23, my parents' 64th wedding anniversary.

His recovery had been good so far, but really slow. An active golfer just two months before, he now was moving about slowly with a walker and a wheel chair.

He hadn't been home in more than two months. My exhausted and devoted mother had been by his side for 10 to 12 hours a day for the entire time.

My sister began crying as soon as I said hello.

"He fell again," was all she could squeak out.

She was Daddy's Baby Girl and I was #1 Son so my sister and I had a peculiar relationship, but I certainly understood why she was so upset. So was I.

Patiently, I asked where he was and what had happened. He had fallen in the rehab facility just a couple hours earlier when he got up to visit the bathroom (even though he was told not to do so without assistance) and tripped over a mat on floor. He'd broken the <u>other</u> hip in exactly the same way.

Sis said my mother was freaking out, and that just doesn't happen. She's been the rock of the family for 60 years, so the thought of her freaking out sent us all into a spiral.

Adapting to a Changing World Brings Even More Opportunity to Serve.

I have an online business. I'm my own boss. With my laptop in my bag, I can do business from anywhere—including the hospital room. I was the only one of my siblings with that kind of flexibility, so I kissed my wife early Sunday morning and pointed my truck toward central Florida, where I could best be of service to my mother and my siblings for a couple weeks.

As my sister tried to arrange a schedule for people to be by my mother's side, I reminded the family how flexible and independent I could be. I'd take the first two weeks at least. Not a problem.

With a family Facebook group established, my daily posts kept all the family and friends informed about the progress and the occasional setbacks. And we kept the Divine stoked with prayers and positive thoughts from around the world.

Amazing gratitude washed over me. Of course, I was grateful for family and friends who were concerned and helpful. I was grateful for a fantastic medical staff, and I was grateful for my amazing wife who supported me from afar while she held down the fort at home.

But here's why I'm truly grateful: passive income. Business systems that work when you don't. Autoresponders that keep your communication lines open when you are out of pocket. And my ability to embrace change.

Just this morning, my wife said something I wrote down and will keep on my desk for a long time: "As my willingness to change increases, so does the speed of my transformation!"

Why Are Baby Boomers So Confused Today?

In our early lives, people tell us to prepare for the unexpected. But if you're like me and most of the folks I know, we think we're bulletproof, invincible. Until we're not. Tragedy strikes, and we see how vulnerable we are. Time becomes the great equalizer. We get old.

My dad was a big, strapping man with a heart of gold, the judgment of Solomon, and the belief that he would live forever. In fact, he kind of had. Having survived seven heart attacks, two double bypass surgeries, and pretty severe diabetes, we didn't really expect him to live as long as he has. He had other ideas, though. He was planning to live a good life, full of joy, sharing it every day with my mother. He made a few great decisions, based on the time in which he grew up.

After 45 years, he retired from one of the Big Three auto manufacturers at just 58, secure with a pension, health insurance, life insurance, and a company-provided lease car. (They counted his four-and-a-half years of military service in his retirement years; that's how he reached 45 years at such an early age.)

Dad was an unusual executive. Because he'd risen through the ranks from a line worker to the night-shift plant superintendent of the forge shop where they made truck axles, he had managed to qualify for the retirement program under the Unite Auto Workers union guidelines.

He opted to keep his union benefits instead of getting the better management benefits package. That turned out to be an inspired decision. Years later, when the company offered him a buyout to jump from the union benefits package and go with the management package, he became resolute in <u>not</u> making the switch, even as they upped the ante with more money for the buyout. ("If they want it that bad, it's gotta be worth more to me," he said.)

Just a couple years later, all those who had taken the management package and the easy buyout money found themselves without many of their benefits. The company, like many of the old manufacturing companies, went through a bankruptcy. Of course, the union benefits package remained in tact, but the management package was gutted.

No health insurance. No life insurance. Reduced pension. And many more benefits lost. Many of the executives with long histories of loyalty to the company found themselves without the very benefits they'd worked all their lives to earn.

People like me born smack dab in the middle of the Baby Boom (between 1946 and 1964) found themselves in a very difficult transition period. Our belief systems were shaken. Our idea of security was very confused.

We straddle time, with one foot in the pension world and the other in a world where it's every man for himself. Some call it the transition from the Industrial Age, when manufacturing was king, to the Information Age, when knowledge, and turning that into cash, took the front seat.

I'm a child of both, as are many of my friends and most of the members of the NAMS Community. (NAMS is the Novice to Advanced Marketing System—the community I established to help Baby Boomers especially make the transition from pension-based lifestyle to passive income-based lifestyle).

Eighty-five percent of our community is over 45. They are all in transition is some way. I love that because they are a serious group of entrepreneurs who love to work, but love to make an impact even more.

It's Our Job to Stay Smart to Take Care of Ourselves and Others.
In this new world, finding a company that is as loyal to you as you are to them is just not possible. And security? Forget it.

The old forms of security do not exist any longer. They never existed outside yourself. The only security that you can truly build is the security you control, and it's a lot of work to do that. It's the most important work you can do, though, because you have more responsibility today than ever before in the history of our country.

Things we never worried about previously—how to find good health insurance, taking care of our parents, living in a society of older people, even resisting our government oversight when appropriate—suddenly have become very important. Surprises, sometimes devastating and crushing surprises, jolt us into a new reality. We find that we have to make adjustments in our lives to accommodate the lives of others, whether we like it or not.

All of a sudden, your plans aren't necessarily important any longer. You figure out how to make a 180-degree change as quickly as possible, with as little disruption as possible. But if you don't have the financial backbone that comes with passive income and automated systems, the chance of losing everything is very real. Passive income and automated systems. That's the key.

Ultimately, It's All About Me.

With four siblings, all younger, I was in the best position to put everything on hold and get myself to Florida to help my mother. She was my concern. Dad was in the hospital. He'd get the treatment he needed, but Mom was going to need someone to make sure she got what she needed: emotional support, daily meals, grocery shopping, and other errands.

My business kept working while I focused on my parents. Of course, there was a hit while I was gone, but it was a hit only to the extent that I had not automated all the passive income streams yet. That just reinforced why I need to build even more automated passive income streams. That's why I <u>only</u> focus on passive income wherever I can find it.

My mother didn't have to worry about medical or financial issues because of the decisions Dad had made. He had prepared a good, if modest, life for her by focusing on decisions that built passive income for them.

The decisions I make for my family must have exactly that same focus, just as yours do. We don't have a choice in the new world, but we do know what's important and why we do what we do. I want my wife to say what my mother said to the nurse before dad went into surgery for his last procedure: "This is the love of my life for 64 years. You take good care of him."

About the Author

As the CEO and chief architect of NAMS (the Novice to Advanced Marketing System), David Perdew has used all his skills as a journalist, consultant, and entrepreneur to build one of the most successful and fastest-growing business training workshops available today at <u>NextNAMS.com</u> and its supporting membership site at <u>NAMSInsiders.com</u>.

The Novice to Advanced Marketing System is a step-by-step training system focusing on Team Training Tools to help novice to advanced business people become even more successful.

David took a year off in 2003 to personally build a 2,200 square-foot log cabin in north Alabama, where he and his wife, two dogs, and a cat live on 95 acres of forest with four streams and 60-foot waterfall.

Connect with David at:

MyNAMS.com

Facebook: facebook.com/NicheAffiliateMarketingSystem

Just Start: The Best Way to Get Something Done Is To Begin

by Dennis Stemmle

I may have been born an entrepreneur. Both my grandfather and father were entrepreneurs. My grandfather was one of the early Roto-Rooter franchisees, and my father followed in his footsteps, purchasing and starting several Roto-Rooter franchises himself.

I grew up on a plumbing truck and at the golf course, a strange and unusual combination that would lay the foundation for much of my life's success. I spent many summers digging ditches in 90- to 100-degree heat, pumping septic tanks, and cleaning backed up sewer lines. This type of dirty manual labor quickly teaches you the meaning of hard work and the value of a dollar.

For my 13th birthday my grandfather gave me a series of six golf lessons. After my first lesson I was hooked, and within six months I was breaking 85 and had won my first golf tournament. I loved not only the challenge of the game, but also playing with the adults and, of course, beating them on most occasions. I learned about life, business, winning, losing, and honor in both victory and defeat, all on the golf course. I also learned that losing was part of a normal process you had to endure to achieve success. I learned how to survive the embarrassing performances that would occur from time to time and ultimately appear in the press the following day. My mom and dad taught me to finish what I started and to apply my best effort, regardless of my current results or situation. I am proud to say I never once withdrew from any golf tournament I had begun, and that commitment has carried over into all areas of my life.

My mom and dad made many sacrifices to create a better a life for their kids; they were strict but always fair. They believed in allowing their kids to make their own decisions and own the consequences of those decisions. I did not always make the best decisions, but that is part of learning and growing up. They always instilled in me a belief that anything was possible if you were willing to do the work and pay your dues. I think the number one thing that holds people back from achieving their dreams is not fear but a lack of belief in their own ability to achieve their dreams. Without a true belief in your own abilities, you lack the motivation and commitment you need to achieve success. It is a lack of belief that creates the fear that freezes people in their tracks. Contrary to popular belief, fear is the result, not the cause, of inaction.

My first signs of any real business acumen turned up when I was just seven years old. I lived in Brooklyn, New York, and if you lived in the city in those days, you would come across a mouse or two (maybe worse) in your basement from time to time. On one occasion, my mom and aunt discovered an unwelcome guest, and with my dad at work, they turned to a seven-year-old kid to solve the problem. I was ready for the challenge. Perhaps more frightening to them than the mouse running around the house was the long line of kids they later noticed in our driveway. Turns out I had the little fellow in a shoe box and was charging the neighborhood kids a nickel for a look. Hey, it was the '70s and a nickel actually had some value then.

Through the years I started many businesses. Some were failures and others were quite successful, even resulting in sales to public companies. In studying what worked and did not work from first-hand experience, I learned you needed a lot more than desire and a strong work ethic; you need a repeatable model built on proven, repeatable systems and tactics.

It was the 1990s, and the Internet was evolving from an email system and online company brochure to something that could transform businesses. It seems obvious now, but back then many folks thought the Internet was a fad and would never replace mail order catalogs, let alone transform business models.

At the time, I was an executive for a major loan servicing company, and one of my divisions was responsible for affinity marketing. In those days we still mailed our borrowers statements each month, and in those statements we would make product offers for things like insurance, travel, and credit cards. These marketing efforts would not just pay for the costs to generate and mail our statements, they would turn a nice profit for us.

I knew the Web could transform this whole industry. I was so excited I pitched the idea to the executive team, and much to my surprise, my excitement and enthusiasm were not shared. In fact, most thought I was nuts; a few even questioned my judgment.

It was my first big aha! moment. At that moment, I realized I was living someone else's dream. I realized my success would be limited by the decisions of these conservative bankers. As a result, I vowed I would make controlling my own destiny my life's mission, and my first Internet company was born. This company would go on to eventually be valued at close to $250 million dollars.

My first e-commerce website sold sports memorabilia. Sourcing product was a big issue in those days, as fraud and fakes accounted for about 70 percent of the merchandise, and the second largest distributor went bankrupt shortly after our launch. The FBI was conducting sting operations, and the media were reporting countless stories about fake autographed memorabilia. This was an early and expensive lesson on the importance of trust in online marketing.

In an attempt to build more trust and credibility, I opened a store in a local mall, held in-person autograph signings, and formed big name partnerships. In solving the trust problem, I allowed my overhead to skyrocket. Though I was making six figures a year, I found myself with no life, working seven days a week, virtually nonstop. I knew there had to be a better way, but I did not have the answer.

Over the next decade I found myself starting two successful software companies for a Fortune 500 company, becoming Chief Operating Officer for a $500 million real estate and mortgage company, and running one of the world's largest online services marketplaces. Despite all my business and financial success, it was not until May 2011 that I would really learn what was important in life.

My wife, Karen, was diagnosed with a rare form of breast cancer. After her recovery we re-evaluated everything in our lives. When you face the potential death of your soul mate, somehow the money you have made fades to the background, as it will not buy you more time. Armed with a new perspective, we set out to make major changes in our lives and focus on what was really important to us: controlling our time and income.

The solution, it turned out, was very simple, and I actually felt quite stupid for not figuring it out much sooner in our lives. Online marketplaces like eBay, Amazon, and JVZoo.com provide a simple and easy way to earn significant incomes.

My first transaction on JVZoo.com took place in 2013, and I was amazed at the quality of product offerings in their marketplace. I no longer needed to create a whole business infrastructure complete with employees, buildings, inventory, and other required fixed costs. I could promote an already-proven product and focus on driving traffic to the products I selected. JVZoo provides the opportunity to maintain your day job and earn while you learn. As you learn and your business grows, you will start the rewarding lifestyle transition to full-time Internet Marketer.

The journey I took was a long one, and I have three pieces of advice as a result. My first suggestion, and perhaps the best piece of advice I can give you, is to find a mentor to shorten the journey. Find someone who has achieved what you want to achieve and buy their books and programs, join their mastermind groups, and attend their conferences. Make the investment and shorten your learning curve. Don't wait until tomorrow, don't wait for a life-altering event. Take action today. If you don't take action today, how will your tomorrow be any different than today?

My second piece of advice critical to success is to stay focused. Every day someone will offer a new product, report, or secret tip that will double or triple your leads, conversions, and sales. It is very easy to get distracted, and distraction is the enemy of your success. My advice is to pick a niche and a mentor and stick with them for at least a year. If you have selected the right mentor, stay focused, and work hard, you will see significant progress and results.

My third piece of advice is on the critical decision of niche selection. I always answer niche questions with a few questions of my own: What problems are you having in your life right now? Do you want to lose weight? Have more happiness? Make more money? Have more energy? Create more passion? Are these problems unique to you, or do you think others face the same challenges? If you solved a big problem for yourself that others are still having, do you think others might want to know how you did it? Of course they would! Here is a simple example to drive home my message.

Let's say your big problem is you have not been able to lose weight. Next, ask yourself, Do others share this problem, or is it unique to me? If you are reading this in the United States, you know that obesity and excess weight are major problems shared by two out of three Americans, so you know your potential market is quite big.

Next, logon to JVZoo.com and buy one of the highly-rated weight loss programs. After your purchase, sign up to be an affiliate to promote the weight loss program you just purchased. Follow the weight loss program, lose your goal weight, and share your journey with the world via your blog and Facebook page. Offer personal tips and lessons along the way and let people experience your struggles and successes. Posting videos is great for establishing and building social proof and connections with your target audience. Provide affiliate banners and links on your sites so people can purchase and share the program that transformed your life right before their eyes. Capture their emails with lead magnets and utilize an autoresponder email sequence to build deeper relationships and drive more product sales. Break your core offer into a series of smaller splintered products to lower the barrier for people to become your customers. Offer related products to your email list, like power bars, supplements, and workout videos to maximize your earnings and extend your list's engagement with you.

I am amazed at the number of online marketers who are successful initially only to see their businesses nosedive in a few short months. The biggest reason is often that they only offer one product and have no splitter or complementary offerings. I do not want to hear how eating these five super foods will help me lose weight three times a week for six months; do you? I don't know of anything that will kill your list and subsequently your business faster than this approach.

Regardless of the niche you ultimately select, the success formula is the same. The formula I have developed and use regardless of the niche is: CAT = TS. I have never before shared this formula with anyone, but this book seemed like the appropriate time and place. The formula states that Credibility, Authority, and Trust will equal Traffic and Sales. I don't care what business you are in, this model will drive tangible growth in your business. To sustain the model, you have to offer value above and beyond what your clients pay for. The outline is simple, but simple doesn't equal easy. It takes a large amount of discipline and craftsmanship to succeed.

In closing, sign up for all your competitors' lists, buy their products, watch their sales videos, read their sales copy, and attend the industry conferences.

Most importantly, commit yourself to take positive action toward your dreams each and every day.

About the Author

Dennis Stemmle is an entrepreneur, author, speaker, and consultant who has literally transformed the way services are delivered online. Along the way he's become one of the top entrepreneurial and online leaders in the world of online commerce. He is the co-founder of Resale Millionaire, a company whose mission is to help 100,000 people create freedom in their own lives by achieving financial independence.

In the last three years, the revenues from the businesses that he personally owns, co-founded, or managed exceeded $100 million dollars. Born in Brooklyn, New York, he holds a Master's Degree in Business Administration and a Bachelor's Degree in Science from the University of South Carolina. He has over 25 years of diverse startup and Fortune 500 company experience.

Dennis lives in Murrells Inlet, South Carolina, where he pursues his passions for golf, surfing, and all things beach and water. He lives with his wife, Karen, and their son, Bradley.

You can follow Dennis on his blog at DennisStemmle.com and get free training on creating your own successful online business at ResaleMillionaire.com. Resale Millionaire teaches you how to simply walk down your street or drive around your neighborhood and acquire items from yard sales, garage sales, thrift stores, etc., and resell those item online for big profits.

Connect with Dennis on:

Facebook: facebook.com/DennisStemmle

Twitter: @DennisStemmle

LinkedIn: www.linkedin.com/in/dennisstemmle/

Robotize Yourself

by Eric Collin

W ho is Eric Collin? I am a French Canadian living in the Republic of Panama since 2002. I was raised by hard-working parents, who taught me that a good life is achieved through very hard work and a lot of sweat. At 14 I started to build furniture with the help of my dad, who had worked as a carpenter in the past.

At age 15, I began to get furniture orders from my parents' friends and was happy to become independent. At age 18, I was making twice as much as my dad by being self-employed rather than an employee.

Since then, I have started several offline businesses and have had more than 200 employees combined. Each business has taught me that you can make a lot of money by hiring people who know their stuff, even if you know practically nothing. Learn a little of everything and hire people who know a lot of one thing. In short, we only must learn to manage people to be wealthy.

At some point I realized that having an offline business is not that great. You are stuck selling locally and have to take care of your employees. At age 35 I began exploring how to make money on the Internet. I bought everything I saw on Clickbank on the subject and attended many seminars in the U.S. This changed my life completely. I discovered the freedom the Internet gives us. I could be making money in a plane, sleeping, on vacation, in my home office— or, simply put, everywhere.

I started as an affiliate of Clickbank. I began making money by building funnels for various micro-niches. I was capturing leads and was becoming a friend to my followers by subtly offering what they wanted, not what I wanted to sell them.

Then I attended an affiliate summit and started to promote CPA (Cost Per Action) offers. Using my funnels I could gross over $500,000 in three months. (I have to tell you, I was fueled by a contest to spend a night at Playboy Mansion. When you find a great reason to do something, you find a way to do much more than you ever expected!)

Having made real money and having gained social proof, I started to teach others how to make money online, starting from scratch. I even conducted three seminars (in Hawaii, Las Vegas, and Montreal). As a team we were helping students make money live, on the spot. They went home with a duplicable formula.

Throughout my life I have been known as the guy who robotizes everything, the guy who finds shortcuts to do things quicker than anyone else. Once I found the formula to make money online, I started to robotize my system. In short, I have created many online courses helping newbie and intermediate affiliates make money faster than ever.

Thanks to all the mentors I've had, I became a motivational coach and mentor myself, working with Spanish-speaking customers. Year after year, I walk the walk with my students, and we make money together.

In 2014, out of nowhere I became a super affiliate on JVZoo. I hit various leader boards. The affiliate earnings became another extra, alongside my product creations, my CPA promotions, and my personal/membership coaching. As you can see, diversification is important.

The Internet provides the best business opportunities for me. Once you get the formula, you can earn money rapidly. Be focused, believe in yourself, and do it. Contests always push me more than anything else. Look for a contest and decide to be a winner.

My biggest project has been RobotCPA, a plugin that has been in use, tested, and improved since 2010. It is a private piece of art that allows CPA affiliates to make $200,000-plus each month. All their secret tricks and formulas are there. It's very easy for newbies and a time saver for expert affiliates. It's time to reach your goals in no time with this secret weapon.

Imagine for few seconds being able to…

- Clone any successful landing page
- Modify any content you want
- Insert your own affiliate links
- Separate your links by countries
- Connect your Prosper202 or similar tools
- Rotate landing pages (100% Split Testing)
- Find the best-selling combination
- View stats of all traffic and conversions
- Top secret features, to keep your competitors from stealing your gold mines
- And much more…

If you are serious about making money online and do not know where to start, your best bet would be to become a member of Academy 777 and use this powerful weapon called RobotCPA.

Academy 777 is where my students can learn just about anything related to Internet marketing. I personally teach students through seminars, webinars, memberships, and videos, so you can't get lost.

I mostly love to teach how to become a super affiliate and to be the best out there. You must beat your competition and money will pour in. At the end everyone wins. You make more money and your clients are happy to get the best products.

In short, I am a product creator, a super affiliate, and a mentor, all at the same time. This has helped me learn new tactics every day and to pass them on to my students. You can learn how to create a product and also how to become a successful marketer with the right mindset.

My motto is: Life is way too short. I must enjoy this life by traveling, making new friends, and discovering the wonders of this world.

Let me give you my best tips to align the stars in your favor:

- Choose a micro-niche you are passionate about
- Build two squeeze pages, add video, and capture emails
- Keep the winner and add new variations constantly
- Send at least 10 follow-up emails (don't sell at first)
- Make sure your followers love you before selling them anything
- The more you give, the more you will receive
- Prepare your funnel in sequence and track where all your followers are in the funnel
- According to their level, send them quality information or affiliate promotions
- Start a contest and reward the participants who send the most leads into the start of the funnel
- Stay tuned with us, as we keep giving great tips and tools to achieve your goals in no time

As I write this chapter, I am sitting at the pool of a five-star hotel on December 31, 2014. As you can see, you too can merge fun with work. I will teach you to work when you want and where you want. No matter where you are located, money flows in when you do things right.

Don't forget to visit my website and grab everything you need to become a JVZoo star too! We will work together to increase your cash flow.

I really value the power of mentors, helping us focus on lucrative projects and bringing them to success. I have paid a lot to be where I am. I was 100% convinced this was the best freedom a man can get. I wish you the same freedom, too.

About the Author

Eric is a product creator, super affiliate, and mentor. A businessman from a young age, he decided to move his business 100% online in 2008. Since then he is crushing it, creating and promoting software and products. Creator of the Academy777, he takes Internet newbies by the hand and helps them earn their full incomes from the Internet.

Eric speaks French natively, as well as English and Spanish. He has lived in Panama since 2002. His main focus is creating automated software to enjoy life and make money on auto-pilot. His last creation is the famous RobotCPA.

Please go to http://Academy777.com to learn more.

Eric Created:

ACADEMY 777: Online education where everyone learns. Want to start generating consistent cash flow from the Web and be free to travel and still make money? Join us and learn fast and easy at http://Academy777.com

RobotCPA: An online platform where you can automate the process of selling CPA offers. You will instantly become a super affiliate at http://robotcpa.com/

Money Loves Speed

by Greg Jeffries

How Did I Get Started?

began just like most other now-successful marketers I know and have read about: I bought several get-rich-quick products and I struggled—and failed—a lot. I will, however, say that succeeding online is fairly simple—not to be confused with easy—but definitely simple. The problem is, we often look for the easy solution, especially in the beginning. There is a point when your business can become easy or does get easier, assuming you organize and set things up correctly, but that's after you've put in the hard work, time, and usually some money.

It took me about four years of trying, testing, failing, and spending lots of money that I didn't actually have, and then paying all of that debt back, until I finally achieved what I would call online success. In reading about and talking to several other successful online marketers, two to four years seems to be about the average length of time for success or the point when a person's business can run pretty smoothly on autopilot, freeing them to do other things.

During my journey online I've bought dozens of courses, upsells, and software. Some worked, some didn't. Most probably could have worked better, if I had put more effort into mastering them. That's another thing—video sales pages often give the impression that whatever you'll learn will provide instantaneous results. What they don't tell you is that it typically takes awhile to learn or master what you're purchasing…assuming that it works in the first place.

A way to cut your number of failures in half is to pay attention to what other marketers are actually doing, not what they're telling you to do. Learn to read between the lines and duplicate what they are actually doing in their businesses and marketing.

My Aha! Moment

Two very important moments in my journey in online marketing have made a huge impact on my success and the way I think. Number one was coming across Tim Ferriss' book The 4-Hour Workweek. I read this before starting online marketing, and it completely reframed my mind. I have always been an entrepreneur at heart, but my big takeaway from the book was the idea of lifestyle design and the fact that you have the power to design a lifestyle that gives you time to do the things you really want. I see online marketing as the vehicle to allow me to design and maintain that lifestyle I desire.

The other major event that impacted my thinking in online marketing was enrolling in Lee McIntyre's Instant Internet Lifestyle intensive coaching program. At the time it cost a lot of money, but in the training I learned something I have not seen taught in any other online marketing training to this day, and it's so crucial. I learned how the backend of sales and marketing funnels work.

The deeper you get into online marketing, you'll learn that most six-, seven- and eight-figure marketers make those large incomes mainly because they have their own products. In the training Lee went into detail about all the basic components you need to create successful sales funnels and how to structure them. His training gave me a strong foundation to later create my first few video training courses, which was my first big success.

My other takeaway from Lee's training was to do things quickly. It's a bad habit of mine (and many other marketers I know) to try to make things perfect.

Unfortunately a product will likely never be perfect, and even if you think it is, you probably left something out you aren't aware of, or something will break during launch.

So it's a better habit to get comfortable with releasing a good product and work at making it great over time. If you wait for the perfect time and for all the stars to align before making a move, it will likely never come. Money loves speed. So when you have an idea, especially for a product, take massive action and see faster results.

The last key to success I'll leave you with is to never stop learning. To this day I've read several books and watched numerous self-help and motivational videos. I try to read at least one new book a month.

What Was the Result of Everything I've Learned?

In my road to success online, I've dabbled in just about everything, and I've actually made money in just about everything I've tried: selling shirts, affiliate marketing, CPA (Cost Per Action) offers, online courses, business opportunities, SEO, email marketing. I am by no means an expert in any of these areas, so from my own experience, if you're someone who wants to make money online you just have to take action and look for unique ways to get exposure and market what you're doing.

As I mentioned earlier, I've bought dozens of products and spent loads of money learning and failing, but doing so has helped shape the way I now market and present my own offers and products. If I had never failed or hadn't had to figure things out on my own, I wouldn't have the understanding I do today. While it's painful and frustrating when you're learning, it's a very important and crucial phase if you really want to appreciate the success on the other side.

It sucks to struggle and to not know how to take action or to feel like you're held back by lack of money. It's frustrating to watch opportunities pass you by before you had the chance to take advantage of them, but you must remember that it's all a learning experience.

At the beginning of my Internet marketing journey, I didn't have a story because I hadn't done anything. No failures, but also no successes. Now I have both, and I use those experiences to help me sell more products and market myself.

Important Takeaways From My Internet Marketing Journey

- Treat what you're doing online as your business. You've probably heard this before, but it's crucial. If you treat it like a hobby you'll only delay your success.

- Always work toward maximum leverage and authority because time is your most valuable asset. Figure out areas or niches you can get into that provide the opportunity for massive leverage but don't require a lot of time, such as email marketing, Kindle e-books, mobile apps, or writing a physical book. (Writing a book requires much more work up front, but it can open the door for speaking engagements for years to come.)

- Always look for new ways to provide value to others. Money is simply a byproduct of value. In the beginning all you care about is money. But once you have money (and I'm not even talking a million dollars) you'll see that money doesn't matter as much anymore.

- Focus on building an audience and then leveraging that audience to fund your dreams and lifestyle. This is where most people mess up. They put a lot of time and effort into non-evergreen niches or opportunities. Sure, you might be able to make a quick buck exploiting the latest Instagram loophole, but it won't last. The most important asset of any online marketer I know is the email list. Start building an email list with your audience and customers. Then build a relationship with them.

- Your #1 goal as an online marketer is traffic. Leverage popular websites to siphon traffic to your website or email marketing list, because traffic is the lifeblood of your online business. Facebook and Pinterest are fun and wonderful, but your main goal as a marketer is to figure out the best way to reach and acquire new customers using these massive traffic sources. Again, without traffic you have no new customers. Without customers you have no business, and then you'll quickly find yourself back at a 9 to 5.

Last, I'll leave you with this quotation, which I feel sums up the effort required to attain success online. It is often glossed over by top-earning marketers. However, they all put in the time, money, and effort to get where they are. You will have to put forth the same effort if you want similar results. Just be consistent and persistent and you will eventually reach your goals.

> *"There are no shortcuts to any place worth going."*
> **—Beverly Sills**

About the Author

Greg Jeffries is a designer and entrepreneur passionate about marketing and helping others succeed online. He enjoys creating simple, scalable, and sustainable strategies, and then teaching those strategies to others so they can duplicate his success.

Find Greg at <u>Imsource.org</u>

Greg Created:

Evergreen Empire is the culmination of everything Greg has learned online. Inside you'll find what he calls "evergreen" marketing strategies, which means they have been around for a long time and will stay around for awhile. He considers them the pillars of online marketing: SEO, list building, and product creation. Greg's goal in this training is to teach you everything you need to know about online marketing in one place, so you can become an independent marketer.

You can find it at: <u>http://www.evergreenempire.net</u>

Never Quit

by Jay Garces, Jr.

L ike all good stories this one starts at the beginning. And like others, this one is filled with drama, suspense, heartbreak, lessons learned, and eventually victory.

I started marketing online in late 1999/early Y2K, right before the "Dot Bomb" occurred. Remember that? I attended a seminar in 1997 in which the organizers promised to teach all about Internet marketing. Naturally, there was a sales pitch at the end for their merchant services, and I bought in hook, line, and sinker. It wasn't until about two years later, however, when I finally put all that knowledge to work and developed two e-commerce sites. Yes, two years later. I procrastinate sometimes.

The sites were instant hits, largely because they sold "As Seen On TV" products that people were already familiar with and because the products could be drop-shipped. I earned tens of thousands of dollars from the two sites. But my love affair with e-commerce didn't last, mostly because of the fickle nature of the search engines and that capricious, three-letter acronym: SEO (which, incidentally, I became quite good at). Adding to this that I also had a full-time job, a young family, and had even gone back to school, maintaining e-commerce sites myself proved to be too time consuming.

So I jumped into affiliate marketing and AdSense with both feet, pursuing that coveted passive income affiliate lifestyle. You know, the one where you just chill at the beach as checks arrive in your mail box. I earned thousands from this, too, and even became a "super affiliate" for one company (temporarily at least). I did this for several years, feeling blessed to be making extra income on the side.

Then it happened. The Big C, also known as cancer. Bummer. To say that I was very upset would be an understatement; I was miserable. I thought my number was up. God was merciful, though. I lived. The butt-whoopin' I took from the chemotherapy and radiation, however, left me physically, mentally, emotionally, and spiritually drained for a long while. To make matters worse, about a year after I finished my treatment, I was laid off from my job.

Since starting online marketing, I had always earned money, but I wasn't doing it full time. Now I had no choice. I had to quickly figure out a way to earn enough income to replace my former job. After all, I had a family to feed. So I did find a way—with a mix of AdSense and CPA (Cost Per Action) affiliate marketing.

I've made tens of thousands with these, too. And all was well until one very popular search engine decided to kill my website rankings with one of their updates. Poof. Just like that, the bulk of my income disappeared as my sites relied heavily on SEO. (Here's a tip: Don't rely solely on SEO. Diversify, and learn paid traffic. You won't regret it.)

That's when I had an epiphany. Why not focus on creating and marketing my own products? I mean, I'd had great success online thus far. I knew how to write creative copy and even how to write code. I also knew I had passion for teaching. All these years, I had been selling other people's stuff. Why not develop and launch my own products and have others sell for me? With my own products, not only would I have complete control, but I'd be able to build a mailing list—the most valuable asset any marketer can have.

Speaking of assets, I've noticed that many folks come into the industry seeking to start with affiliate marketing, but they fail miserably. Affiliate marketing is a good business model, but a superior one is product creation. It's higher in the food chain, so to speak, and provides real, tangible assets you can sell. Furthermore, as a product creator you have a massive affiliate sales force selling for you instead of the other way around. So my best advice to you when coming into this industry is to start off as a product creator. Then promote someone else's product to your mailing list of buyers (which, incidentally, you've already developed by promoting your own products). Make sense?

Now where was I? Oh, yes. I decided to dive right into product creation and launching. As destiny would have it, around that time a well-known marketer released a training and coaching program—on what? Doing product launches!

I remember thinking, "Wow! God is on my side." I purchased the training and coaching program and started learning. I quickly created an e-book and packaged it with software I had developed months earlier and launched it on a JVZoo competitor site.

Bam! It was a hit. I sold about 300 hundred total units and was immediately hooked. I then began planning my next launch, but I became terribly distracted and didn't get around to my next product launch until about eight months later. This time I created a product named CPA List Code, detailing a simple method I've used to build a mailing list using Cost Per Action affiliate offers.

It was an instant hit. It even received accolades. But something was missing. The platform I was using was okay, but I wasn't getting the mileage I wanted in terms of sales, name recognition, or promotional support.

That's when I started looking into JVZoo. Everyone I asked kept telling me that the platform was superior, and all the big-name, serious marketers were there. I fixed my eyes on JVZoo for my next product launch.

Alas, dear reader, you may think that this is the part of the story when success rains down like sunshine on a Miami morning, and I walk away with a seven-figure pay day. It isn't. As with all things in life, there's a beginning and an end, and a short time after the second launch, I lost my dad. Several months later I lost my abuelita (grandmother) and two other family members, one right after the other. Around the same time, I was even forced into bankruptcy.

I was distraught. I took a long break and even considered quitting. But the entrepreneurial fire in me began burning stronger than ever. It was being fanned by the memory of my father, who by my age had already owned and sold two clothing factories and employed dozens of people.

After taking those hits, I had a choice to make: quit or start anew. Freak it. I decided on the latter. It was drilled into me during my time in the Marines: never quit. So I picked up where I left off and focused on getting my first JVZoo product launch.

And I did it, just this past September, and it was my highest-grossing product launch yet. As a matter of fact, my dear reader, as I write this, I have a launch underway on JVZoo. The product? An updated version of CPA List Code. The last time I looked I had over 200 front-end unit sales and climbing.

Now JVZoo is my silent partner. There my name is recognized, and the affiliate promotional support is second to none. Remember, all you need is one or two big-name marketers promoting for you and you're in bankville.

Using JVZoo has gotten me more sales not only because many big-named marketers search that platform for offers to promote, but also because it's a well-recognized and trusted brand. I get to be associated with that just by being on JVZoo. With JVZoo by my side, I'm paving the way for online marketing and business success.

For me, dear reader, this story is far from over. I have my eyes fixed on great things. Who knows? Maybe I'll even begin a startup. Stay tuned, dear reader, stay tuned.

About the Author

Jay Garces, Jr. is an Internet marketer and copywriter who is quite good at product creation. You'll often find him unapologetically using his sales copy skills to help others sell more of their products. You can contact Jay via his site: http://www.JayGarcesJr.com

Connect with Jay on:
Facebook: facebook.com/josegarcesjr

Jay Created:

CPA List Code Reloaded teaches Internet marketing newbies a slick way to build a mailing list, while getting paid to do it. You can find it at: http://cpalistcode.com

The Aha! Moment

by John Racine

I had been working in hospitality as a human resources professional for several years when my boss sent me to a motivational seminar. The seminar was attended by thousands of people and boasted hugely famous keynote speakers, including Rudy Giuliani, Zig Ziglar, and Colin Powell.

The last speaker of the day was a guy named Stephen Pierce, who talked about using the Internet to make money. Though I had been sitting in the same seat for over eight hours, something told me to stay and listen. Everything he said made absolute sense to me, so I signed up for his program.

The next thing I knew, I was an affiliate marketer using the Internet to drive traffic to offers on Amazon and another CPA (Cost Per Action) company. I got into it and started building websites for countless affiliate and CPA offers. I was really excited when the affiliate sales commissions started hitting my PayPal and bank accounts.

During this time, I began getting emails from other marketers about topics like Amazon, SEO, link building, webinars, and so on. I wanted to invest in my education, so I purchased several of these programs in my quest to become the best marketer I could. But when I filed my taxes that year, it dawned on me that

I had invested a ton of money in various programs, and that money went to the creators of each of those products and programs.

Talk about an aha! moment. I did some basic math on these purchases and realized the creators were making a lot of money by sharing what they knew. That was the moment I knew I wanted to be a product creator and earn money sharing what I had learned.

I started researching many of the top product launches and vendors and what they were doing to achieve their results. I looked at Anik Singal, Lee McIntyre, Stephen Pierce, Dan the Internet Man, and others. It became very obvious these guys were doing massive launches and had a ton of experience, but they all were saying the same thing: "Share what you have learned. You don't have to be an expert."

It was hard to wrap my head around this, but I eventually embraced it and released my first product, an interview I did with Lee McIntyre. I was pretty nervous talking to Lee one-on-one, but in the end, I started selling my product on the largest community website for Internet marketers, the Warrior Forum.

I got a real education about the back end of my business during that first launch—mainly that I needed to have a back end. I did not have any additional offers or any value-add products to enhance what I was providing for my customers.

Over time, I created more products and added them to the back end of that first product. I added a program on product creation, showing how I had created that interview with Lee. I even took a stab at WordPress plugin development. I learned the hard way that I wasn't good at managing my developer and providing a clear vision of what I wanted. But I didn't give up on plugins, at least not then.

I had also been playing around with Amazon selling, rather than promoting as an affiliate. This is called Fulfillment by Amazon. I sourced products that Amazon then sold as well as handled the payment, the shipping, and the customer service.

I was doing pretty well with Fulfillment by Amazon and created a product around it and put it up for sale on the Warrior Forum. It was my biggest launch at that point, and JVZoo had not yet been created. Boy, I wish it had though.

I put a lot of time into planning that launch, and I created what I thought was a pretty cool membership site. I used Optimize Press and Wish List Member to create it. I added a few things that no one else was doing at the time, such as Non Member Pages, used to upsell pieces of the funnel to people who normally wouldn't have access to those pieces based on their previous purchases. I also used custom video on the registration page to show customers how to upgrade their membership with a new purchase. And I used the membership sidebar menu for banners advertising my other products and select affiliate offers.

Several customers of this product were impressed with the setup, and word spread. Before I knew it, I was being hired by people all over the world to create their membership sites. Russ Ruffino even called, asking me to help his consulting students with their member sites, one of them on launch day.

I soon became known as the Wishlist Go-To Guy and a membership site expert. I didn't set out to be that, but I ran with it. Before long, people told me I should put what I knew about membership sites into a product. It had been a while since my last launch, so I started putting the Membership Manifesto together.

I had worked behind the scenes on several high-profile JVZoo launches, handling membership setup, testing, and more. This would be my first solo launch on JVZoo.

I decided make it the most comprehensive resource available for integrating Optimize Press and Wish List Member. I also opted to highlight different ways to create membership sites using simple scripts, coding, and free plugins.

One of my earlier products ended up on a black hat site, which affected my sales. So I also chose to demonstrate how to add simple protection to products and to deliver them through a membership site or even a protected content area of a website.

I began putting the program together. Then a few things happened that were both wonderful and painful at the same time. These circumstances would eventually add a lot of value to my Membership Manifesto.

The highlight of the Membership Manifesto was going to be the ninja strategies I used to create sites with Optimize Press and Wish List. Well, Optimize Press 2.0 was about to release when I was also about to launch. I chose to add brand new Optimize Press 2 content to the Membership Manifesto. It made sense for me to add Optimize Press 2 since I knew many people would upgrade to 2.0, myself included, but many more would continue to use the industry standard Optimize Press 1.0 version.

I had been working with John Thornhill, a legendary marketer, who recommended I also add a live training course on how to get paid to create membership sites so customers could see an easy way to make some money online before having a list. It was a no-brainer; I added it. Great suggestion, John!

I put this program into the JVZoo system, whose team was awesome. Bryan Zimmerman personally helped me during a holiday weekend so everything would be ready for launch that Tuesday.

JVZoo is pretty awesome because it handles customer payments, affiliate payments, affiliate contest tracking, adding buyers, autoresponders, webinars, and so much more. My launch went off without a hitch, allowing me to focus on customer service and affiliate recruitment. I was excited I got to share my knowledge with so many people through the Membership Manifesto.

Shortly after this launch, I attended my first Internet marketing event: Marketing Mayhem Live 2014 in Orlando. Let me tell you, I had heard for years that attending this event would really grow your business, but I now know that to be fact. I got to meet and socialize with many of the people I admired online and in JVZoo.

I came away from the event reinvigorated and excited to take my business to the next level. In online marketing we often work alone or in isolation, and getting to spend time with people who are smarter about marketing and online business really helps up your game and be more successful. Big shout out and thank you to the JVZoo team for putting the entire platform and community together.

Thanks guys, YOU ROCK!

About the Author

John Racine spent his younger years in New England and moved to Orlando, Florida, after college to work at Disney World. He became involved with Internet marketing after hearing Stephen Pierce speak. He has experience with affiliate marketing, product creation, membership sites, and general business, and he's devoted to helping people achieve their goals with their online and offline businesses.

Connect with John at:

JohnRacine.com

Facebook: facebook.com/jjracine

Twitter: @johnracinejr

John Created:

The Membership Manifesto is the most comprehensive training available on creating high-value, easy-to-manage, and profitable membership sites. Optimize Press and Wish List Member are featured throughout the program, but it also includes how-to's for free membership plugins, WordPress, and standard html pages. If  you want to create a site and develop a large customer base to earn residual income, then you need the Membership Manifesto.

Get the training at: TheMembershipManifesto.com

An Easier Way

by Kelly James

I wrote this chapter just for you...because this is where you need to start. No, I'm not just trying to drum up sales, though if you are going to pursue this industry for a living, you must understand that a great marketer does just that. It's the main reason we are all in this book, after all.

The secondary reason, though, is to give back. When you've finish this chapter, you'll see there was little about me and very much about you. It's the shortcut I wish I'd had when I first started.

I am Kelly James, part owner of Hit & Run Marketing. I started making money online in 2000 on eBay, and I instantly fell in love with it. Of course, back then you could win an auction, immediately re-list the item using the previous auction's pictures, and make an easy 50 or 100 bucks within hours. It boiled down to watching for items that were listed under the average going price. After awhile I was buying and selling products in the musical instruments and gear categories. When the masses caught on and it was no longer easy to make money, I moved on.

Next up were high-priced e-books. I once paid $297 for one, and yes, it was worth it. I learned as much as I could, and that was the start of an eight-year downward spiral. I was always looking for the next thing that would make everything perfect for me to start making money online. I finally came to my senses and began making small affiliate review and info websites.

I also did odd jobs from the forums, like graphics, articles, keyword research and lists, videos, shell sites, and more. I became the biggest propeller head you ever met. The pay wasn't always great, but it taught me an important lesson about this business, and it eventually led me to JVZoo.

You see, people hired me to do the bits and pieces they could not, whereas I was trying to do everything myself, leading me to believe that online marketing was hard work, even though it's not. All you need is a product to sell and an audience to sell it to, or an affiliate product or service—it doesn't matter. It needs to be good but not great and not perfect. You don't need to create every step of the process. You just need to know what the process is and where to get it done if you can't or don't want to do it yourself.

This made me ask the question: Why isn't there one place where all this information is organized in one nice spot? A kind of 'make money online Wiki-Rolodex-Tutorial site,' with just the meat and potatoes, from A to Z. There would be tons of proven business models laid out step by step and where to have each step done for you. It would be a place where the guru 'secrets' would no longer be secret, creating a level playing field.

After thinking about how great this would be, I realized I had the idea for my first big product to launch on JVZoo. Imagine you've bought a course and then get stuck; you search their forum and ask questions, then search for a solution on YouTube, but you're still stuck. Not a problem. Just go to WebTurfWar.com and find your main category. Click it to view the tutorial videos and PDFs, or just pick a name from the listing of reputable sites or people who do that type of task. Now you're back in business. So are you looking to launch a JVZoo product, start a membership site, learn SEO, create viral videos, build sites, flip sites, or do local marketing for your brick and mortar business?

In case you were wondering: No, you don't have to purchase any particular product to use our site. You can easily start there. There are many great products that can make you money, and you may want to try one of them.

When we launch Web Turf War in March, you'll be able to do all these things and much more. In the meantime there are some super ninja money-making videos on the site to hold you over until the full site is ready—including one killer JVZoo secrets tutorial. There's also an in-depth video explanation of what will be on the site since I can't tell you everything here. The video will show anyone how to make or get a product, software, or service ready to sell on the Web, as well as all the places to sell it, including JVZoo.

You're going to find that you don't need to create any specific type of product for JVZoo. There's value in a single video if done properly. Or a product on time management, a pack of headers you made in Gimp, an e-book on building 2.0 backlinks, a video on creating articles fast and easy. I've purchased all of these types of products.

If you're not sure where to start, just head over to our site and watch the only video of its kind on this subject. Then you will know what you want and how to do it. That is our gift to you! It's all free for now, so get there while you can.

I wish you the best of luck, and I hope to see you on our site. Maybe someday I'll be pitching one of your products to our list. Either way, you know where to go if you get stuck.

To Your Super Ninja Success,

Kelly James

WebTurfWar.com

Web Turf War: Vol. 1.0 (Pro)

HitAndRunMarketing.com

About the Author

Kelly James has been working/marketing online for over 14 years starting online (as a hobby) with eBay. Although she loved that avenue for making money online she realized there were far greater opportunities and easier methods available.

While on this leg of her internet career she learned the coveted skills of creating websites, landers, web graphics, content creation, and conversion testing among a few others.

This also led to a greater understanding of matching online work with personality or "The Real Journey" as she likes to call it. She says this was when she found the greatest success online and that getting her internet feet wet was the best decision she ever made so go get your feet wet.

The Mobile Awakening

by Kevin Zicherman

My name is Kevin Z, founder and CEO of brick&mobile, a world leader in mobile marketing reseller solutions. Over the past five years I've trained over 7,000 mobile marketing resellers in over 30 countries and powered thousands of mobile marketing campaigns around the world.

But it didn't start off easy. To understand where I've gone, it's important to know where I came from.

When I was young I was a sales guy. I loved marketing. I loved advertising. I wanted to make TV commercials. I loved the idea of convincing people to take certain actions through the means of marketing.

My dad, on the other hand, wanted me to be an economist. He wanted me to be a business guy, so I started studying business economics. After a while I thought, "Forget this math. Go with your passion."

I chose to study marketing, and I excelled at it. I knew that's where I wanted to be. And I learned to not let anyone else dictate my future.

After I graduated from university, I spent eight long years working for "the man," helping make other people rich. Being an entrepreneur at heart, I knew something had to change.

Until early 2011, I worked for Canada's largest media company, selling millions in Internet and mobile advertising to multi-national Fortune 50 brands. I was #1 in sales on my digital sales team and was pulling in more than anyone else with a double territory.

I began to see some fascinating trends in the industry. Newspaper and television sales teams were missing their targets, their clients' budgets were being slashed, and sadly, they were getting laid off. It opened my eyes to a massive opportunity: all the media money was moving to mobile!

At the time I was living with my girlfriend. I wanted to propose to her, but we weren't married yet, and we had no kids. I figured if there were one point in my life when I should take a leap of faith or walk the plank, it was now. There was no other time.

So I did it. With literally no back-up plan, I quit my job. My girlfriend had just completed her studies, so it was a time for us to be free. We traveled around Asia for four months, and I proposed to her at the top of Victoria's Peak in Hong Kong. During this amazing around-the-world journey, I had time to reflect. I realized I had no wires holding me up anymore.

Nobody was telling me what to do, but I also didn't really know what I was going to do. I just knew that I didn't want anybody to tell me what to do anymore. I had jumped off the cliff without a parachute.

I thought about how the companies I'd worked for were putting most of their eggs into the mobile marketing basket, and I realized I needed to do something in mobile. I just knew it had to be done and that I was the person to do it.

I had four months to pull myself together, while on the trip of a lifetime. I came back engaged, with a wonderful future ahead of me. I was sitting at my desk with my sharp pencil and my empty notepad, thinking, "Now what?"

For the first year and a half, I tried everything to get my business on track. I went to seminars, I read constantly, I worked on my marketing tools. I purchased products on the Warrior Forum. I found free reports. I tried everything under the sun to make money online, to no avail. I had the tools, but I was missing the focus.

I knew I needed the help of an expert. Someone who could tell me, "Been there, done that, and this is how I turned things around." I decided to talk with a friend, who ended up becoming my first mentor. (I later learned that it's okay to have more than one.) He is a very smart guy, someone I met through the one of the biggest agencies, and he's well-respected and currently very high up at Google.

During our first meeting I told him how I had quit my job and what I had been doing for the past year and a half. I didn't tell him how dire the situation was, but I said I was still looking for focus. I also told him I saw a future with mobile and that I was thinking about selling mobile websites to local marketers.

He told me to go with what I was best at. Then he asked me, "If money were not an issue, what would you do? If you had all the money in the world, what job would you work at?" I responded, "I wouldn't work!"

He then said, "Seriously. If you had to do this job, and in exchange for doing this job you'd get paid a certain salary, what would it be?" After I actually thought about it, I said I would sell. I would get out there and sell because I love marketing. I love sales. I love helping people.

He then said, "You said it yourself—local marketing is massive. Mobile is a big part of that. You quit your job because of mobile."

The light bulb finally went on inside this thick brain of mine. During the whole year and a half, even though I was working, I wasn't building affiliate sites doing what I enjoyed. I was running around in circles trying the 'affiliate get-rich-quick, make money in your sleep' kind of thing. I finally realized that all I'd done was waste my time.

My friend told me to follow my dream. So I started building mobile websites manually. I first built them in WordPress, then I started building them in HTML. I was selling them to local businesses, but I was spending a lot of time building the sites and not enough time selling them.

I told myself, for this really to work I have to build a process, a system. I have to build a platform to build these mobile websites. I was on the fence about it, though, when I remembered my mentor's words of wisdom: "Follow what you're good at, and focus on one thing."

He helped me realize that for a year and a half, I'd been letting other people set my agenda with bright shiny objects and emails. He made me realize that I had to set my own agenda. He made me realize that this was what I was good at, so I needed to invest my time and money into building this platform. I would no longer be the jack of all trades, master of none.

As I started to build more systems to allow for growth, I decided to build a real company instead of a one-horse business. Given my success, I wanted to replicate my system for others, and I chose to specialize in resellers. I knew I could change their lives just by training them on what I do, and if I do what's right for them and I help them succeed, the money will come.

It may come as a surprise, but there are still misconceptions about mobile marketing. Despite the warmer reception it's been receiving, there are still many "experts" who are either ignorant of mobile marketing or just don't have a clear idea of its definition and usage.

The biggest misconception is that mobile marketing is not really needed. Many companies are still looking to traditional marketing strategies, such as radio, print, and large-scale promotions and campaigns, to increase interest and revenue. They hope these methods will still pique interest and generate powerful word-of-mouth. But if examined closely, mobile marketing is an extension of word-of-mouth. Companies that invest in mobile marketing use Facebook campaigns, mobile email promotions, and even QR coding to share their products with a 1.2 billion strong demographic who use their mobile devices on a daily basis. Any company not willing to invest in that kind of audience is wasting a great opportunity for growth.

Approximately 70 percent of small businesses have invested more in mobile marketing this year, and of these small businesses, around 84 percent enjoy tremendous growth in revenue, customer engagement, and visibility.

Believe it or not, mobile phones now outnumber computers, signifying that mobile marketing is the next area for advancement in marketing schemes, as well as one of the strongest and most powerful marketing tools for any business. It is well on its way to making billions of dollars.

Mobile marketing is a popular and appealing form of advertising used by both small and large businesses to keep in step with today's fast-paced world. Since just about everyone has a smart phone, it's a great way for your company to get in touch with your target audiences and convince them to become your newest customers.

Research shows that over half of all smart phone users look up products on their phones, with over a third actually buying the product on their phone. This proves that the mobile marketing strategy you use works to bring in more sales and profits—if you do it right! My point is that all businesses need a mobile marketing plan or they will lose potentially larger profits.

So to answer whether you can really make money using mobile marketing... the answer is yes! ...as long as your systems are in order.

About the Author

Kevin Zicherman is a seasoned marketing professional with over 15 years of experience in corporate, startup, and entrepreneurial-based digital Web and mobile ecosystems.

Kevin is currently the CEO of brick&mobile (www. brickandmobile.com), a full service mobile marketing company specializing in turnkey reseller programs and White Label Mobile CMS solutions.

Having trained over 7,000 mobile marketing resellers in over 30 countries, Kevin's passion for mobile innovation and sales training is a driving force for his successful mobile marketing partners and local resellers worldwide.

Connect with Kevin at:

Facebook: facebook.com/kzicherman

Twitter: @kzic

Linked: linkedin.com/in/kzicherman

Kevin Created:

Brick&Mobile specializes in providing the most robust, full-service mobile marketing reseller programs available today. Powering thousands of mobile marketing campaigns around the world, brick&mobile's proven strategies, workshops, and marketing platforms deliver cost-effective solutions that are easy to launch and maintain.

By integrating a complete suite of turnkey services, such as mobile websites, Wi-Fi marketing, NFC tags, mobile wallet loyalty programs, QR codes, and SMS text message marketing, brick&mobile is the only mobile reseller partner you need.

Learn more at: www.brickandmobile.com

Becoming a Traffic Hero

by Patrick Anderson

've lived what most people would call a strange life. I'm constantly asked, "What do you do?" It seems like every time I get a call from a family member or friend, they ask what I'm doing. I usually answer, "Just chillin,'" or "I'm at the gym." Let me explain.

For years I traveled the world with my circus acrobat group, performing for millions of people and selling over 100,000 of our DVDs by hand—or, as we would say, out of the trunk of a car. Throughout this time I thought, "We could make a lot more money if we could just get our DVD in front of more people." Now, I just do not like to write, so a website or blog was out of the question. So I said, "Hey, let's check out this social media thing."

First, I suggested we check out YouTube. With YouTube we could make use of video to communicate our messages online. I was eager to impress people through online videos so I wouldn't have to travel so much.

I first started shooting videos with my phone. The first videos were not that good, but with time I got better. I was able to shoot clear videos that many people enjoyed viewing, and I came up with really good content. Videos are heard as well as watched, so I was keen on making sure the audio quality was also great. I was able to achieve this by eliminating background noise when shooting the videos.

Once I started seeing good results, I developed a system that made the process simple. I was able to get our message to millions more people, allowing us to earn more money and thus allowing me to work from home, promoting and selling various products online.

It was a great time for me. I was able to stop traveling and spend more time with my beautiful wife. Did I mention I got to spend more time with my wife?

I uploaded the promotion videos to YouTube and shared them on other social media platforms, where people viewed them and became fans. I primarily shared the YouTube videos on Facebook, Instagram, and Twitter. I made sure to utilize Facebook well. I began learning about how to create posts that people would love to share, eventually making their friends my friends. It worked great because Facebook encourages people to share.

This was the beginning of my online career and the creation of my new program, 21 Day Traffic Hero. With this program I will share what I discovered along my amazing journey. I'll share tactics and strategies that lead to a lot of traffic, which leads to growing your online business with a few simple tactics. I look forward to sharing these strategies with you this summer when the 21 Day Traffic Hero launches.

About the Author

A professional athlete turned website marketing specialist, Patrick Anderson has a proven success record driving online traffic to his clients' websites and social media profiles. He offers expert services for small- to medium-sized businesses using traditional websites, Facebook, YouTube, Instagram, Twitter, Pinterest, and more to promote their messages.

Before any work begins, Patrick meets with each of his clients to learn about the company and understand their goals. Patrick has worked with many business types, including restaurants, day care centers, and chiropractic offices. Using information gathered in the initial meeting, along with his own knowledge of current online trends and technologies, Patrick creates a plan with action items designed to increase traffic, capture followers, and ultimately increase profits.

As a National Association for Fitness Certified (NAFC) personal trainer, Patrick possesses inside knowledge of the health and wellness industry and offers a competitive edge to other personal trainers, fitness centers, and gyms looking to increase their online visibility.

Prior to starting this business, Patrick worked as a professional circus acrobat for 15 years. Being an acrobat gave him the opportunity to travel the world and even perform for Nelson Mandela in South Africa—an accomplishment he's extremely proud of.

He is the author of several e-books on topics related to both fitness and Internet marketing strategies for driving traffic. When he is not helping his clients harness the power of the Internet to attract customers, Patrick enjoys exercising and staying in top physical condition.

Patrick is grateful to work in a business that allows him to combine his passions for fitness and technology. In the future, he hopes he can use his specialized skills and knowledge to help many other businesses reach their online marketing goals.

You can learn more about Patrick at 21daytraffichero.com.

Success Through Partnerships

by Rex Harris

I started dabbling in the idea of a home-based business using the Internet in the fall of 2000. At that time, I was working as a kitchen manager at a Big Boy in Petoskey, Michigan.

I soon realized that there was more to selling stuff online than just posting a few ads and hoping for the best. With the help of a friend, we covered the entire northern tip of Michigan with pull tab fliers. It was amazing to see the fast response those fliers generated. Then sales began to follow.

In January 2001 we were informed that the company providing our products was closing its doors. I guess that's what happens when you sell computer systems to people with bad credit.

At that time I did the only thing I knew how to do—I returned to commission sales. After eight months of effort and selling anything I could earn a commission on, I was offered a management position, which was great...until two weeks before Christmas in 2001, when I was given notice that the retail store where I was employed was closing its doors forever.

The thought of finding another job was daunting, and it was time to make a decision regarding how I would make money. The choice was simple: go back to work or finally sit down at the computer and do whatever it took to turn a profit online.

I used my first unemployment check to start a small advertising business and have been working online ever since. When I woke up one March morning to find "Notification of Payment Received" staring at me from the computer screen like a big present on Christmas morning, I was hooked and couldn't wait to make that happen over and over again.

Every day I posted hundreds of ads. I didn't mind because the money rolled in each time I did one of these "ad-a-thons." The problem was, on the days I didn't do this, I wasn't making money. I knew there had to be a way to do it without spending so much time.

Without even knowing what I was doing, the idea came to me to log into PayPal and copy the email addresses of everyone who had purchased advertising from me. I sent an email promoting a new advertising package to everyone who had already purchased from me. It resulted in my first thousand dollar day.

That was my first aha! moment—the day I learned the value of having a list of proven buyers. As a result, I began collecting email addresses as part of my daily routine. Then I wanted everyone else to know how to do it, too. To add value for those on my list, I started offering daily webinars to teach this technique. The workshops were a hit!

My second aha! moment came when I realized that by occasionally offering a special during these workshops, I could make thousands of dollars in just a couple of hours. Again, I wanted to teach it, so I began demonstrating how to do online workshops.

Over the years I've fine-tuned the training process. In August 2014, a couple friends and I teamed up to launch the Academy of Home Business.

I would love to be able to say that my work in online marketing has been all sunshine and roses, but that's not the case. For many years, the struggle was greater than the profit. The struggle came not so much with the business side of things, but from within myself.

My biggest error early on was approaching things with trepidation. I wasn't afraid to ask people for money, but I was afraid to ask for it in larger amounts. My self-talk sounded something like, "People aren't going to spend that much money for this or that."

After connecting with my first real mentor in 2007, I realized that type of thinking was ridiculous. The point was driven home when the help

I received from this mentor resulted in over $16,000 in sales in less than two weeks.

Why am I sharing these thoughts with you? For the same reason I've been doing what I do, every day, for the last ten years. By God's amazing grace, as I write this, I'm sitting at our poolside table as the sun begins to peak over the trees. I have a fantastic home, a great family, and a short commute that I wouldn't trade for anything.

I decided to be part of this project to share my advice with anyone who wants to receive it. I wasted a lot of time over the years doubting myself. There's a fantastic chance that if you want this enough, you can make it happen.

What I have learned is that it's easier when you work with others and partner up. Every successful project I've been a part of has been with a partner. The best way to find partners is to attend events. Attending events has changed my life, especially over the last two years. As an example, since my first Marketing Mayhem event in August 2014, my income has tripled! How? Making friends and working together!

Here's a tip you can take away from this: Networking events happen throughout the year in just about every state in the U.S. and countries around the world. Major networking events like Marketing Mayhem, as well as smaller local ones, are a great way to get in, get your feet wet, and start branching out. Do a Google search for "network after work," find an event in your area, and go! It may require a little driving, but it's worth it!

Based on what I've learned and witnessed, those who become prosperous in our workspace work together. We see it all the time, in all forms of business. You don't have to know everything to be part of a project, just your part. That's the point! You can accomplish amazing results in less time when you work with the right people.

About the Author

Rex Harris is a happy grandpa and dad with an amazing wife and family. He started dabbling in online marketing about 15 years ago and started taking it seriously in 2001 after being laid off. He enjoys sharing what he's learned with others to build relationships.

Connect with Rex at:

Facebook: facebook.com/rexharrislive

Twitter: @rexharrislive

Website: AcademyOfHomeBusiness.com

Phone: 239-692-1468

Email: askrexharris@gmail.com

Rex Created:

The Academy of Home Business is a membership site dedicated to helping other Internet marketers, network marketers, and home business owners find the best answers and solutions for the businesses they want to build or the products they want to promote. Our site includes video training, live training via workshops and webinars, and personal access to people who are running profitable home businesses.

Learn more at: AcademyOfHomeBusiness.com

The Epiphany

by Ricardo Rodriguez

Phase 1: Reality Check

I n 1994 I decided to try my hand at college life. I attended classes and
worked part time in the college office as a file clerk. I worked hard every
day. I made great efforts to impress my boss. I always arrived early and was
the last to leave.

I had a coworker who was the opposite. He was always late, never started
his work load on time, and always left early. One day my boss handed me
two paychecks: mine and my coworker's. I had the privilege of delivering his
check to him, as I was going to pass his office anyway. Of course, I noticed
how much his paycheck was, and I was flabbergasted. I had been working so
hard but received the same pay as a person I perceived to be a slacker, for lack
of a better word.

I immediately approached my boss and asked for a raise. I just knew
the answer would be yes, seeing as I had been working so hard and putting
in so many hours. You can imagine my disappointment when I heard the

words, "Sorry, not possible." All I could think was, "Are you kidding? Why do I get the same pay as someone who doesn't put in near as much work and commitment?"

Well, you know what happened next. Yes, you guessed it. I extended my hand and said, "Have a nice day. You will not see me again." In my eyes they were losing the best employee they'd ever had. It's good I left with my self-worth intact, because that resignation led to my reading a life-altering ad.

Phase 2: The Ad

After the disappointment of walking away from a job that I was actually fond of, I didn't just sit around and twiddle my thumbs. I knew there was something better for me out there, and I was determined to find it. So the search began.

I came across an interesting advertisement that I never imagined would change the course of my life forever. It was a general ad that simply stated, "Warehouse manager, start from the ground floor up, learn inventory, office work, paid daily." It sounded interesting enough, so I called and set up an interview.

I headed into a decent-sized office and waited patiently for my name to be called. I entered the office and gave the best interview I had in me. Later that day I received the call offering the position and was told to report the next day at 8 am.

I entered the office sharp as could be, wearing comfortable shoes, a nice suit, and a fresh hair cut. They paired me with a gentleman who would take me on 'a day of observation.'

I got in his car, and we traveled to the busiest area in New York City. I was wondering, when would I learn the warehouse part of all this? We got out of the car, and he went to the trunk and filled a duffle bag with loads of cheap Chinese goods. We were going to go business to business selling these items until the trunk was empty. You can imagine the puzzled look on my face, but I went along out of curiosity.

It was a 90-degree summer day, and I was wearing a suit. I was just a shy kid from Puerto Rico, living in Brooklyn, New York. What was I doing? Well, this, ladies and gentlemen, was my first introduction to sales.

My trainer sold every piece of merchandise he started with, more than 70 pieces. I told myself, if he can do this, I am sure I can. We headed back to the office, where I would be interviewed a second time. At that moment, I made the decision to stay and try my hand at sales.

For two days I continued to observe. On the third day I had my own merchandise, and it was my turn to sell. I entered my first door and said, "Hello, can I get a soda and a Snickers?" I paid for it and walked out. I never even offered what I had.

My trainer asked, "How did it go?"

I said, "Oh, they didn't want anything, so I bought a snack instead."

The second door I walked through, I told them I was nervous, it was my first day, everything is 80 percent off, and do you want anything? What do you know, I made my first sale!

I tried my hand at this for the next three months, making 20 dollars a day. I have heard every "no" that there is to hear. My favorite was, "Get a real job." But things changed.

Phase 3: The Epiphany

I woke up one morning and said to myself, "No one will sell more than me today." When I got in to the office, the boss called all the leaders into a room. I was not called in, as I was not yet a leader in anything except selling the <u>least</u> amount of goods each day.

But I wasn't going to let that get me down. I interrupted their leaders meeting and put $100 on the table. I said, "No one is beating me in sales today. Who's in?" Everyone laughed and took the bet, since I had not sold much of anything for the last three months.

I was feeling confident, and there was $800 up for grabs to the winner of the bet. I made one thousand bucks that day and was the #1 seller for the next two months. Talk about a confidence booster. Who knew you could be the director of your own destiny?! You can actually decide how much money you want to make, go for it, and achieve it.

Phase 4: Business Owner?

When you achieved the leader title, you could start building a team. It would be a small group at first, but eventually you would be in a position to run a warehouse of goods yourself. I was only 21 years old and felt quite apprehensive about taking on such a large task. My manager sat me down for a heart to heart—you know, to give me encouragement to move on to the next level.

I will never forget what he said: "Don't be afraid to take the next step. If you screw it up, you screw it up, but at least you learned something." I took the advice and went for it.

Two weeks later I got incorporated, and at the age of 21, I was running a $5 million a year company. I opened two locations, one in Brooklyn, New York, and the other in Washington, D.C.

Phase 5: Bumps and Bruises

Did I run into bumps in the road? Of course! I didn't know all the things I needed to have in place to keep my business running and flourishing. After all was said and done, I had a great ride, but I had to start from the bottom again. I did a lot of reflecting. Where did I go wrong? What should I have done differently? Where was I lacking? How could I do better?

Phase 6: Education and the Company You Keep

I have learned that having positive, goal-oriented people in your corner is good for your business. I have come to understand the value of trustworthy and business-minded people being a part of my life. There is nothing better than unselfish people who are willing to lend their experience and expertise for your benefit. I found it very useful to have a mentor.

From my mentor I learned that a very important step to running your own business is education. You have to educate yourself on the products or services you are offering. You must know the demographics you want to reach. You need to understand what I have come to call 'The five key components needed to be successful in your business.' They are:

1. A primary company, a legacy company. A company that you can work on for the next two years and will pay you for the next 50.
2. A lead generating system. You need to generate leads for your company to bring in new prospects and clientele.
3. A mentor. Michael Jordan was the best, and even he had a mentor. A mentor can give you direction and guidance. You will have help to stay on the right track.
4. A system to manage your business. This will help you see what is working for you and what's not working.

5. An educational program. This is a training program that will educate you on how to manage your business. You will learn how to speak to clients and how to retain them.

Phase 7: Helping others

From my experiences I have created a script that I call the Ultimate Script. I have used this script to my own benefit, and to the benefit of others. I have been successful at helping others get more comfortable on the phones gaining and retaining clients. Rejection is a part of business, but with the script, fellow marketers have gotten more comfortable dealing with the ups and downs of this business.

I have been teaching fellow marketers, regardless of whether they are in the same primary company as me. I have found that giving back is what helps you become successful. I use my own example of ups and downs to help others avoid certain pitfalls. If I have learned anything, it's that you can't get to the top on your own, and stepping on people to get to the top will only lead to failure in the long run.

I have been sharing my story for years now. I have trained others as a business and sales coach. Success is more enjoyable when it is shared. I have enjoyed being a mentor and will continue to do so for as long as I can.

About the Author

Hello, Ricardo Rodriguez here. I'm your second income consultant.

Like so many people, I grew tired of worrying how the bills would get paid every month. I grew tired of working a job I didn't really enjoy and that I knew would never create the life I wanted and deserved. There was nothing worse than going to bed every night feeling that what I was reaching for was so far away.

So I decided to do something about it. Believe it or not, that decision alone did wonders for me. It gave me a feeling of control and hope that I never felt working for somebody else!

Now I know why. Working from home has been an absolute blessing. It's taught me how to work smarter rather than harder. It's helping me make more money, and at the same time create more time to enjoy it. It provides me the opportunity to meet other people just like me and help them create the life and lifestyle they dream about.

If you're friendly and have a goal in mind, I'd love to work with you. In fact, there's a team of people behind me who devote every day of their lives to helping good people succeed with this incredible opportunity.

Whether you have a lot of experience or none at all, a lot of time to invest or just a little, it's all good! Our company, our team, and our proven system work with what you've got—and help you bring about the results you're looking for.

If you have any questions, contact me! If you have any concerns, let me know! If you're ready to go, I'm right there with you! I am living proof that this business really can change your life!

Connect with Ricardo at:

seethisamazingvideo.com/products/

Facebook: facebook.com/Salu3599

Twitter: @Salu3599

Confessions Of A JVZoo Junkie

by Robert Blakely

This is about my journey as a JVZoo junkie! I hope you find my story both educational and informational as you journey toward success as an affiliate or network marketer. But no matter how much you learn from myself or others, the only way you will truly succeed is by taking actions and applying the information learned. So let's get started!

Through life I have considered myself an all-American kind of guy. I first caught the entrepreneurial spirit when I was 16 as I delivered the local newspaper. When I was introduced to an hourly wage job working at McDonald's at age 17, I quickly learned the value of trading time for money.

After graduating high school, I entered the U.S. Army and learned a great deal about team building and leadership development. However, it wasn't until I left the military and experienced a great twist of fate in meeting a new friend that I truly learned the value of writing my own paycheck. I learned that our biggest obstacles to success will always be lack of knowledge and lack of confidence. We are our own worst enemy!

I never attended college, but I often think of those who do go to college, spend thousands of dollars, and still don't enjoy their profession. That path never interested me. My advice instead is to determine what you're passionate about and learn how to monetize that passion!

For you to be successful at affiliate/network marketing, or even monetizing your passion, it takes some time and money to learn the best ways to succeed. It's like going to college for affiliate marketing. Obviously you will want to choose what to be involved with wisely in this stage of the profession.

I enjoy being like a professor for affiliate and network marketing. I help people cut down the time and money investment considerably by simply providing information I have learned over my lifetime.

After personally learning all the types of marketing known to man, I found affiliate marketing to be a great pathway to future success. Think about it—when someone gets their start in sales, they generally sell someone else's products and services. They next learn how to create products. They develop and promote their own products and services with the intent of solving a problem in the marketplace. But how are people to know the problems in the marketplace if they are not even in the market? Well, they must first get involved and take action.

I have found that many people don't have the right communication skills for making the sale. In fact, many people are afraid of the word 'sale' because of our natural human fear of rejection. These people typically don't take the correct actions toward success; in fact, many take no action at all! When we learn to embrace rejection and learn from the process, we become better at understanding what a sale is. When you have your aha! moment, you will understand what I mean.

After years of direct marketing experience, learning sales psychology, and training others to be effective communicators and understand customers, I decided I could do the same coaching online. I could make even more connections if I had the right tools to accomplish the mission.

At this time, I was introduced to a website called JVZoo. It became an addiction I will always be thankful for. Using what I learned from network marketing and many of the products available on JVZoo, I set up my own websites and funnels for my businesses. I have been able to build some incredible relationships through network marketing events as well.

My first year in direct marketing/affiliate sales, I earned $50,000. If you take the time to learn the industry and how to solve problems in the marketplace, it can be a very rewarding way to generate income. I personally love JVZoo for the access it provides to great minds and to great products to use or sell to others.

So what can a JVZoo addict tell you that will bring positive value to your life?

First, find out what you're passionate about. This can be a difficult task; many marketers don't really know what they want to do. In fact, I always explain that network marketers are taught incorrectly, as far as the steps and processes we need to be successful at online marketing. We must first find our passion, as passion is something that can't be taught!

So what is it that you're passionate about? When you discover what you're passionate about and then monetize that passion, you will do extremely well in network or affiliate marketing.

Second, set up a website to catch names and emails using an autoresponder service. When you have a list of clients to market to, your job of selling becomes a lot easier.

Finally, provide a service that others in the marketplace need! If you weave baskets but aren't talking to people who need baskets, then you won't sell many baskets. So find a way to engage with your target market. Create a splash page with video and an autoresponder form that will entice people to provide their information to your list. Then build a relationship with all the people on that list.

The better people know you and the more they like you, the more they will trust you. Do not betray their trust! Give people a free offer or report that directly solves a problem. Let them know you are there to help, and provide the best service people can find in your niche.

Then make sure you're fulfilling people's needs. It's very easy to discover what people need by simply talking with them and listening intently. After you have identified a need for a specific product, simply provide it. This can be done easily with affiliate marketing and JVZoo. Find the correct product, apply for an affiliate relationship with the vendor, then share your affiliate link with the person who needs it most.

At the same time make sure your lists are segmented for specific products. For example, network marketers who are into Web development may want to receive offers for WordPress plug-ins. Thus, don't send those people an email about health products. Do your best to not send offers to people who don't need what you are offering. This will kill your list by making those people uninterested in what you sell, and it could also give you a bad name in the industry. Find the best products, purchase them for your personal use, then decide which are best to promote to certain lists.

Most of all, become a product of the product! Don't sell products you have no real interest in just to make money. The more support you can provide, the better it will be for you and your clients.

In review: find out what you're passionate about, create a website to capture names and emails, and then work on "know, like, trust." When you build a trusting relationship with your list and offer people value, you will see great results.

In closing, I would like to leave you with a phrase I learned from my drill instructor in the military. "Good, better, best, never let it rest, until your good is better and your better is best!"

I hope you've found some value in my words and that they motivate you to achieve success. Thanks for reading.

Robert Blakely

TheRandRMarketing.com

About the Author

My name is Robert Blakely, and I am a JVZoo junkie! I am 45 going on 26 because I never want to grow up!

I was born in the west Texas town of El Paso on July 19, 1969, the day before man set foot on the moon. Growing up I had an entrepreneurial spirit. I started as a newspaper carrier, and worked my way into management at every job I decided to work.

I started training others how to do their jobs when I was just 17 years old, which gives me a lot of experience training others on how to be successful. I also spent five years in the U.S. Army, which taught me leadership development.

I am an affiliate marketer, and I love to sell products of extreme value! My goal is to assist others in finding their success paths quickly! Let's connect!

Robert Blakely AKA (The Blakester)

facebook.com/TheBlakestersMadness

Twitter: @RobertBlakely

TheRandRMarketing.com

Primary Business:

theblakester.avisae.com/

Email:

robertblakely.theblakester@gmail.com

Robert Offers:

balance™

Optimal Hydration, Health and Vitality Formula

Prime hydration, peak health, and increasing your body's vitality are more accessible now than ever. OptimALL Nutrition balance™ is an all-natural, organic mineral supplement that balances your body's pH through mineralization. balance™ promotes increased hydration, mineral consumption, and nutrient and phytonutrient absorption.

Key Benefits

balance™ Your Hydration

A healthy pH balance preserves the integrity of our digestive enzymes, allowing our bodies to assimilate and absorb essential nutrients from our food.*

balance™ Your Health

balance™ delivers more than 70 vital trace minerals, which increases energy and metabolism, reduces joint pain, improves immune functions and decreases chances of heart disease.*

balance™ Your Vitality

Balancing your pH levels and delivering essential minerals directly to your cells helps your body dramatically reduce internal stress levels. It strengthens the brain, strengthens the heart and efficiently controls insulin levels.*

Find out more at: theblakester.avisae.com/

From Job Slavery To Freedom In Less Than 3 Years

by Walt Bayliss

From chained to a desk, working 80 hours a week, to financial freedom, in under three years. This is my story.

I was doing well. I was doing very well, actually. I held a corporate sales job with a computer software company and was entrusted with running the division internationally. I <u>was</u> my career, and I was proud of it. I didn't realize I was a slave until it was nearly too late.

I met my wife when my company sent me to London, and we were married shortly after. When the company transferred me back to Australia, my wife came too, and life continued on at a hectic pace. That pace continued while our marriage grew and we found out we were expecting our first child.

I was excited, but truthfully I didn't know what to expect. Pregnancy must be tough, but I wasn't around for it. I was traveling, working, and continuing on what I thought was the best path. Because of that focus, I took just three days and one single weekend off work when our daughter was born. I returned to my desk while my wife and new baby girl were still in the hospital.

Shortly after, I had a massive change of perspective. I remember it clearly. It was the day a sledge hammer in my head repeatedly pounded the question, "What the heck am I doing?"

The same desk and office that had motivated me now frightened me, as I pictured the bleak future to come. So I started looking for a different way to make money.

At the time I was reading <u>Retire Young, Retire Rich,</u> a book by Robert Kiyosaki, who is also the author of <u>Rich Dad, Poor Dad</u>. He said that whatever you feel passionate about can become a source of income for you. That made it easy for me—you see, I was passionate about looking after my finances.

That may seem a strange thing to be passionate about, but that fanatical approach to my personal finances had gotten me out of a very deep hole earlier in my life. When I was in my mid-20s, I was earning good money but not holding onto a single dollar. I was a financial mess, owing more than I could pay and not thinking about the future.

It was so bad, in fact, that when a $600 phone bill arrived in my mailbox, I didn't have the means to pay it. The red letters across the top of the bill informed me that if the payment wasn't made shortly, serious legal repercussions would follow.

In desperation I asked my best friend, Neil, a very successful real estate agent, to borrow the $600. To his credit and my huge advantage, he said no. He said not until I teach you how to manage your money so you don't find yourself in trouble again. He sat with me and talked about a concept called cash flow. Neil didn't leave my side until it was truly knocked into my head.

I became fanatical about cash flow, to the point where I could pinpoint my exact bank account position six months into the future because I knew every single in and out of every single dollar that was going through my account.

This knowledge got me out of financial trouble, and it also meant Neil had a very different answer for me the next time I asked to borrow money.

I called Neil six months after the phone bill incident and asked him to lend me $10,000 so I could buy an undervalued business I had seen for sale. I had a strong plan to turn the business around to profit and then sell it. Neil happily gave me the $10,000 overnight, when he didn't give me $600 earlier. And I did go on to sell the business for a tidy profit.

So I was fanatical about cash flow, and I was working for a company that employed computer programmers who could build software. I was on the sales team, so I did not have any technical skills when it came to programming, but my good friend in the company, Ian, had all the skills I needed.

A partnership was born when I asked Ian if he could build the very program I had in mind and he gladly agreed. He would do the programming side and I would do the sales side. We both thought it was a match made in heaven.

I'd love to tell you that everything just took off for me from there. I'd love to tell you that, but it isn't true. You see, I had a unique product and a good product. I expected sales to come flocking in, to wake up in the morning with an account full of cash. But that didn't happen, not by a long shot.

In fact, nothing happened, absolutely nothing. So much so that I nearly threw it in. I nearly gave it up at that point as a lost exercise, an "Oh, well, I gave it a shot" kind of attitude.

But in desperation, I thought I'd try and throw some money on advertising, so I went to Google, and I typed in "how to advertise my product." As you can imagine, there were millions of results. One result, however, caught my eye. It promised free advertising of any product.

I thought to myself, "Well, that can't be a bad thing." So I clicked the link and found myself on a site where all I had to do was sign up, view other people's ads, and in exchange they got to view mine.

In theory, it's a terrific practice. So I clicked on some ads and built up my credits, then put in the ad for my product, again expecting to see wads of cash in my account the following morning.

By now you know the story, there was no cash, but there was activity on my site. I saw visitors materialize from the air. I thought to myself, "This is the beginning. Now that I have people coming to the site, I know I'm in the right place. All I need to do is get enough of them to come, and I will make sales."

But this is the part where I'd like to talk to you about finding the correct audience. The people who were advertising on the site and the people who were clicking on my links and my ads were, in fact, just looking for traction for their own ads. I didn't realize that for a long time. Actually, as we build toward the success part of this story, the fact that I didn't realize it actually led to my biggest aha! moment.

You see, I started pouring money into these advertising sites—and there were plenty of them. Every time I clicked on a link, I found new advertising sites offering the same thing, a place where I could build up my credits and advertise my own product. I was still of the opinion that if I had enough people visit my site, surely some of them would convert to sales.

As I joined more and more and more of these sites, I started paying money instead of clicking to build up the credits. You can only click so many times in a day, and the alternative was to simply buy upgraded memberships, which allowed me to send my ads without waiting around for the credits to build up.

The money started to flow out toward the advertising, and it's true, the traffic to the website went up, but the conversion ratio was so terrible that for every $50 I was making in a sale I was spending close to $500 to generate that sale.

This was when I had the true light bulb moment. I realized that the very place where I was spending money was, in fact, the place where I could be making money. I was spending a lot of money on advertising, and I could see other people doing the same thing. I thought to myself, "If I had one of these advertising sites, which all seem to follow the same template, then people could pay me to advertise their products instead of me paying them to advertise mine."

This is where my success really took off. I Googled for the template of the advertising websites that I'd been using to run my advertisements. So many of these sites looked and felt exactly the same, so I knew there must be a template that people could purchase to set up their own sites. I found the template I was looking for, and the entire system cost $25.

With a little bit more research, I found out how to get this type of site up online and ready to open the doors. And so I began. With graphics that I created in the free paint program from Microsoft, and absolutely no experience in this kind of site whatsoever, I opened the site and began posting ads on the other sites. This time, instead of advertising my finance product, my ads pointed back to this new advertising site.

This is when I came across the concept of affiliates. My new site had a built-in affiliate system. It was lucky for me that it was built in, as I didn't know what an affiliate program was. But those who did understand the affiliate program started sending it out to their own databases. They received 50 percent of every sale they sent me, and boy, did the sales come. With these affiliates sending me thousands of visitors, the very first day the site was online we made over $1,000 in sales. The sales kept coming over a period of about a week, and the money coming through the door absolutely blew my mind.

What was more important for my long-term growth was that now I had a building database of my own. The very next week, when somebody else opened another one of these advertising sites, I was able to send an email to my database about the new site and again picked up thousands of dollars in commissions from sending my traffic across to somebody else's site.

At this time, I bought out my partner, Ian, from the finance software, to ease my conscience that I hadn't paid him for any of the hard work he'd done. He was paid, and the foundation of my first successful venture online was firmly in place.

I duplicated that same site again and again and quickly realized that people love to jump onto something new. The attraction to each new site was fantastic for about a week or maybe two, then people were onto the next one, looking for the next influx of free traffic.

This worked really well for me for about a year, where I continued to build new sites to promote other people's sites. Money was coming in quickly from this new source of income. I even branched out into other systems in the advertising space, made them my own, and launched them. Our first $25,000 month was a massive windfall.

Around this time I started seriously thinking about giving up on my corporate career. The income from the advertising sites was tempting me toward that decision. As I grew in success on the Internet, I started getting invited to people's businesses to talk about their own websites and about what they could do online. And when the people I was speaking to pulled out their checkbooks and wrote a check for $5,000 without batting an eye, I thought, "This is where our future really lies." The money was so easy, as people were looking at their own websites, not really understanding what they could do to generate more traffic.

One weekend I signed up to be an exhibitor at a business conference and offered website services in exchange for a monthly fee. We rode over $25,000 of recurring monthly income right there on that weekend. "This is real income," I thought. It wasn't dependent on launching new sites. I could simply take on clients and work with them and continue having the money come in month after month. Because of this newfound direction, my corporate job was actually costing me money, as I could better spend that time meeting with clients. I needed to quit.

You may think this is the sunshine part of the story, but it would actually lead into the darkest chapter of my life.

As I worked toward the quitting date of my job and looked at the new income from working with clients, I decided I would sell the advertising sites to give us a safety net and buy a house before starting off on this new venture. That's exactly what I did. I brought in $75,000 for the sale of the advertising websites. Not bad, considering each of them had paid me as they were built and were sold as an asset only a year and a half later. It's a great lesson to learn that any valuable real estate online or offline can be sold at future value, so it's worth building them very well.

The other great lesson came for me at this point as well. As I sold the goose that laid the golden eggs and poured myself into working with clients, I realized that I had traded one full-time job for another. That was okay, as I was working for myself and felt like I had more control over our future. But then things on the Internet changed quickly.

Google released updates that made ranking sites extremely difficult, where it once was extremely easy. Overnight the success I had built up for my portfolio of clients showed statistics that looked like they fell off a cliff. Page 1 rankings simply disappeared, traffic dried up, and people were looking to me for answers. Not being scared of hard work, I hit the books and tried to find the answers, too.

I looked and I looked and I looked but couldn't find the answer to my problems. I cancelled the ongoing monthly fees coming in from the clients, as I was no longer able to deliver results I was proud of and didn't feel right about continuing to charge while I struggled to find the answers. I turned off the sales team, as I didn't want any new contracts coming through in an environment where I couldn't achieve the desired results.

This was the picture: no new sales coming in, no ongoing monthly revenue, no income from the advertising system. I was really in trouble.

With a new mortgage, a wife, and a baby, I suddenly found myself facing financial devastation. Money was going out fast and not coming in at all. It very nearly broke me; in fact, I had less than $10 in my bank account. I said to my wife as I went out for a run that if we hadn't made any money by the time I got back, I would have to go and get a job, as we were simply out of money.

I asked for help from the universe during that run. I remember nearly begging for a signal that I was on the right path. Knowing that if we hadn't made any money by the time I got back I would have to give myself over to a lifetime of corporate slavery, I started that run in a very depressed state. But the universe heard me, thankfully, and when I returned from the run we had made a grand total of 22 cents.

Twenty-two whole cents. It wasn't enough to even buy a lolly from the shop, but it was the signal that I needed for a confidence boost. It encouraged me to look back at where I had found success in the past, and I repeated my light bulb moment from before. Where am I spending money? I could immediately look at that and find an answer for the situation we found ourselves in.

At the time I was spending it on the Warrior Forum, trying to buy products and shortcuts that would help me get the results I needed for my clients. I wondered if flipping my spending to income would be something I'd be able to do again.

During the process of trying to get results for my clients, one of the things that <u>was</u> still working was buying an aged and page-ranked domain name, and immediately sending links back to the sites I was trying to rank. To do this, I was scouring the GoDaddy database for domains that had expired or were expiring soon that I could buy for pennies on the dollar, sites that already had age and authority from their time on the Web.

As part of the process of trying to make life easier, I had found a way to automate that database hunting. I'd written, through some research, a program called a macro that did a lot of the copying and pasting that I needed to do to get the results quicker. Without much experience I offered that product for sale on the Warrior Forum, as what was called a Warrior Special Offer. I called it PR Powershot.

That was a Friday, the day I went for a run with less than $10 in my bank account. That very same weekend, we made over $20,000 in sales of that product. (It still sells very well today.) And everything changed from that weekend.

I started finding out how to approach JV partners in this new world of the Warrior Forum and of software. Taking the skills I had already learned from affiliate promotions, I started driving traffic to other people's matching offers as well.

Around this time, in 2011, my second daughter, Ivana, was born. By then, I was a full time dad with a growing business. All the while I had been building software products.

I need to stress that I don't have any technical skills in this area, but these days we have over 40 skilled software developers on staff, contracted as outsourcers in our company. I have learned how to put my thoughts down on paper and how to present those thoughts to people with the right skills. I pay them the fee they asked for, so they can build out the concept I had in my mind to an end product.

We repeated the process with different products, such as WordPress plug-ins. In each launch we attracted new and bigger affiliates. The same people who were doing the development work covered our support desk, so users could ask questions of the people who actually programmed the software. This one thing changed my life, as I was no longer spending six hours a day on support tickets.

The team continues to develop the programs I ask for and continues to support our clients as our database grows with new clients every single day. Learning how to target those audiences, instead of spending money on advertising to people who aren't interested, has allowed us to build our income to a point where we are self-sustaining.

And our business continues to grow, as new ideas and new technologies come into the marketplace. We're always looking at different ways to improve the quality of people's lives. We're building products and technology and always keeping the customer in the front of mind. We have a good foundation (just under a million in sales in the last year), but we are not done yet! New products will come and new ideas are being built.

If I can help you on your journey with a few key points, they would be these:

Look at the places where you are spending money. They can be your biggest income sources. Can you do it better? Faster? In an easier way? People will pay for that.

Always write your ideas down, as you never know how much value they have.

Work with people who have the skills you don't, and pay them what they need to be paid. Their knowledge and experience will take you farther.

Make sure the people you listen to have walked the path you want to walk.

And the biggest one—never, NEVER ever give up! You (yes, YOU) can do it, too.

About the Author

From a corporate slave to financial freedom in less than three years, Walt Bayliss now runs a successful software business from his laptop anywhere in the world.

He spent more than 18 months traveling Europe with his wife and two children while his business grew to be bigger than when he left. Now based in Australia, Walt's business continues to grow from more than 3,000 customers globally.

Specializing in business software, Walt's business success is due to the people around him. He says, "My roles are the ideas and the relationships. Everything else is done by my talented team of people all over the world."

Connect with Walt at:

UniversalMediaOnline.com

Facebook: facebook.com/waltbayliss

Twitter: @umomedia

LinkedIn: au.linkedin.com/pub/walter-bayliss/17/764/960/

Walt Created:

RunClick software is the biggest secret for anyone involved in online marketing. It allows you to hold fully interactive webinars, run evergreen presentation funnels (selling your product for you, without you even being there!) and more. Used by more than 9,000 people to run their presentations, webinars, and training, RunClick software is the must-have tool for anyone looking to present and make sales online.

Find out more at http://runclick.com.

Get Ahead Of Traffic Trends

by Ronald Edwards

I t all started the night before I graduated high school, quite a few years ago. I was born and raised in a small town in Michigan and didn't have a clue what I was going to do with my life. Luckily my father had moved to Florida several years earlier after divorcing my mother and started an automotive repair business. He'd offered me a job working for him. The Internet didn't even exist back then.

The day after graduation, I moved to Florida and worked at my dad's tow truck company for about two years. It was interesting work, but very physical, and you had to be on call almost every hour of the day and night. Dad eventually sold the business to a new owner, and he and I didn't get along, so I left.

Back in high school I took a course in computer programming and got rather good at it. At the time I hadn't seen the bright future it promised (a missed opportunity on my part). I was more interested in electronics, and unfortunately I pursued that career for quite a few years after quitting the towing business.

I had always been interested in electronics and became very good at repairing televisions. I moved to the Tampa Bay area several years later and started my own TV repair business. I did that for around 15 years, until 2003, when TVs became cheaper to buy. I knew the TV repair business was doomed, so I started looking for other ways to make money, and I thought the Internet would be a good choice.

The big difference between an offline business and an online business is the overhead. When I had my TV shop, I had to pay rent on a building, electricity and water, a vehicle (truck payments, gas, and insurance), local licenses and fees, and employees. At the end of the month, after I paid for all those things, what was left was mine. With an online business, most of those expenses would be eliminated.

I had gotten my first computer in 1997, when I found out my friends were getting deals on things that I couldn't because I didn't have a computer. To be honest, when I got my first PC, I didn't know where to start. I didn't even know how to turn it on. I finally found the power switch in the back but literally didn't know what else to do with it. The computer terminals I'd used to learn programming back in high school were completely different.

I joined AOL, and my dial-up modem was so slow that when I clicked a link, I would go make a sandwich, and by the time I got back, the page would have just finished loading. When I got an email I was so excited. Does anyone remember those days?

There was no training whatsoever on how to make money online, but finally around 2003 I began learning how to build websites. I built one for my TV repair business, a very simple three-page website, using an HTML editor called FrontPage. Nowadays, we don't even use HTML because of CMS (content management systems), but there are some advantages to understanding what's happening in the underlying code.

I spent my evenings in the webmaster forums, trying to figure out how people were making money online. I learned about a thing called AdSense, where you could run ads on your websites. When people clicked the ads, you made money. People were making a lot of money this way, so I started creating sites. I built over one hundred websites, about five of which really took off.

I started getting a lot of traffic, and life was very good for several years because I was making serious money on autopilot. The best thing was that I didn't have to talk to anybody or sell anything. No customer support, no returns, no shipping, no merchant accounts.

Unfortunately, when Google started the Panda updates, my traffic dropped to 10 percent of what it had been. Shortly after I was barely making enough money to live on, so I decided to make money online without Google. I started learning about paid traffic.

What I liked about paid traffic was that it was scalable and predictable and didn't have anything to do with search engine algorithms. The downside is that, because you are paying for traffic, you really have to watch your conversions or you will lose money quickly.

In hindsight, I should have looked at conversions years earlier when I was getting free traffic, because even though I made a lot of money, I'd had over 27 million visitors in about six years. I probably could have made 10 times more money had I known then what I know now about conversion rates.

Recently I started my own podcast to help people learn about Internet marketing and to not make the same mistakes I've made. I also started buying and selling products on JVZoo. I believe it's the best platform for people to get started making money online, because you can start by selling other people's products. Eventually you can learn to create your own products, and others will sell them for you.

Over the years I bought every new product I could get my hands on, and I went to literally dozens of out-of-town marketing seminars. I estimate I spent over $100,000 on self-education. At this point I believe it was well worth it, but you have to be careful not to be distracted by all the shiny objects, which can divert you from your main goal. The point I'm trying to make here is, don't try to do more than three or four things at once in Internet marketing.

I believe that you should get ahead of traffic trends to capitalize on them. In the Internet game, traffic equals money. The more visitors you get, the more money you make. For instance, at the time of this writing, Facebook, Instagram, YouTube, and SoundCloud are all experiencing an increase in traffic. (To see if a site's traffic is on the rise, go to semrush.com and enter a domain name.) These sites allow you to post for free traffic, or you can pay for it to get more exposure.

Another thing to take into consideration is mobile. Mobile traffic is on the rise and will eventually take over desktop and laptop computer traffic. With mobile traffic you get a much higher click-through rate on ads, as compared to a desktop computer, because the banner ad takes up more space on the screen. The conversion rates are much lower, however, mainly because it's difficult to input credit card information on a small screen. Apple and PayPal are working on one-click solutions on mobile devices for this problem, but I won't get into that right now.

Another thing to consider is that most offline businesses don't have a clue how to market online. They are too busy trying to run the business to learn how to attract more business online. This is a huge opportunity for anyone who can make their phone ring. A popular business model is to charge clients for phone leads, using phone tracking software. It can record the calls and even send an invoice for the leads automatically.

The bottom line is that there has never been a better opportunity to make a good living online than right now. With all the tools and training available, you can get started right away. The hardest part is deciding what to sell, a product or a service.

In the 10+ years I've been marketing online, I failed a lot, but I learned from the failures. I look at a failure simply as test data. After all, Thomas Edison failed at inventing the light bulb over 1,000 times. But then he found a way that did work, and he lit the world.

About the Author

Ronald Edwards is originally from Kalamazoo, Michigan. He moved Florida at age 18 and worked for his father as a tow truck driver for two years. He then learned to repair TVs and started his own TV repair business. Since 2004, Ronald has been making a living online, selling Web traffic and health products.

Connect with Ronald at:

MonsterResource.com
Facebook: facebook.com/monsterresource
Twitter: @monsterresource
LinkedIn: linkedin.com/in/monsterresource

Taking The Internet By Storm

by Todd Gross

My path into Internet marketing is a bit "creative." In short, as early as the first grade I knew I wanted to be a weatherman on television. I actually did go into that profession, becoming proficient on camera. When I semi-retired in 2006, I took that talent and leveraged it to jump into affiliate marketing and creating video-oriented products. I've stayed on a steady course ever since!

How did I end up as JVZoo's #1 affiliate for 2014 (and all time)? I think it has to do with my personalized, focused approach.

I actually started blogging and website creation back in 1995, before blogs actually existed. I rapidly became a 'guru' in the astronomy niche by writing product reviews straight onto a website, and I began trading telescopes and eyepieces as well. Meanwhile, my television career was soaring, and I became the chief meteorologist at the NBC affiliate in Boston.

When I left that position at the end of 2005, I came up with a crazy idea: What if I brought my weather forecasts to the Internet? That's when the roller coaster ride began.

In order to monetize my online forecasts, I started to explore Google's AdSense program and quickly found Joel Comm's best-seller, <u>AdSense Secrets</u>, which had recently been published for the first time. As I explored AdSense, I naturally started receiving emails from marketers pushing the latest and greatest AdSense training products. Boom, I was thrust into the Internet marketing world!

Two thoughts ran through my head:

1. <u>This</u> was where the money is
2. Where's the video?

Here's where it got interesting. I already had a green screen setup to do my weather forecasts online. Why not do video work for these crazy marketing types who were flooding my inbox?

In order to catch the attention of one such marketer, Derrick Van Dyke, I actually did a live-look green screen video promoting his current product at the time, Affiliate Cash Secrets. To my astonishment, he actually answered my email to his generic email address. YES!

Derrick was so impressed with my ideas of doing stand-up video to market products online, he suggested we start a service, which we called Squeeze Videos, to allow other marketers to create video squeeze pages in various niches. To my knowledge, this was one of the first concerted efforts at bringing these now-commonplace video squeeze pages to the market.

With a fresh new list of leads borne from our successful launch of Squeeze Videos, in October 2006 I began my very long and remarkably steady journey of promoting other people's related products as an affiliate.

One thing I discovered quickly is that it's crucial to team up with those who can cover tasks I was not qualified to do on my own. Initially I was helped by bigger marketers, such as Derrick and also Harris Fellman. In exchange I would help with their video work and promotions.

In fact, as so many successful marketers do, I continued to team with others, and I found some of the best…or somehow they found me. Linda Nash, Mark Lareau, and more recently Luann Beckman and Shannon Murphy, are just a few of the friends and colleagues who took up my slack, helping me build my list by coming out with fresh products on Clickbank, Warrior+, and eventually JVZoo. I quickly became a top, sought-after affiliate and product spokesman.

At the same time I continued to work part-time in television, doing weather reports and announcing on stations in Springfield, Massachusetts, Salt Lake City, and CNBC. However, it became crystal clear that I needed to stay focused on my video marketing, as this would eventually bring the success we needed to stabilize our lives. (My very supportive wife, Ava, was by my side through all this.)

However, there was a problem. From the outside, it appeared I was doing well, but since I was trying to replace a big market television salary, I had run into debt like so many others who go into this not-so-stable business. As the years went by, I only barely kept myself from going under, and I kept losing a remarkable number of subscribers on my lists. In late 2013, I finally made up my mind to try four new marketing techniques, which eventually shot me to the top:

1. Create more products to build a list of buyers more quickly
2. Narrow down my focus to mostly video-oriented products to avoid buyer burnout
3. Speak directly with my list by having them see me on camera before promoting my products or other people's products
4. Put myself on the sales pages of other video-oriented products by offering my video-spokesman services

These four strategies worked together in 2014 to literally triple my sales. Whether it was my own product, or I was promoting someone else's, the familiarity that the buying audience had with me made them more comfortable purchasing from me than ever before.

Previously, in a typical promotion I might sell anywhere from 100 to 200 units of a low-cost $17 product, and never more than 600. In 2014, I hit 1,000 units many times over, culminating with VideoMaker FX (2,000 sales) and Easy Sketch Pro (3,600 sales in one day alone).

In 2014 I also released very targeted products that solidified my renown as a video marketer, such as Green Screen Profit, and I teamed up with the Easy Web Video owners on a regular series of promotions for their line of products.

It's no coincidence that all these products were part of the JVZoo marketplace. Part of my success has been due to being able to quickly go with the flow, offering special pricing, discount coupons, and other incentives to boost sales and affiliate involvement. The JVZoo marketplace offered the perfect set of tools to optimize sales this way, and it continues to be an easy, affordable, and super-quick way to get promotions out there for my own products and affiliate promotions.

In my August 2014 presentation at JVZoo's Marketing Mayhem, I shared my #1 secret: To really connect with your audience, you should put yourself between that audience and the product in question, whether it is your own or an affiliate product you are promoting. You can do this with a review video, a stand-up video, or any other kind of video that you see fit. It is important to present yourself as the gatekeeper of that product, and the best way to do it is with video.

About the Author

Todd Gross, the "Weatherman Marketer" has been involved in online sales since 1994. However, his main profession was TV meteorologist, working at stations like the NBC affiliate in Boston, the Today Show in New York, and occasional live hurricane coverage on CNBC. Todd was even portrayed in the major motion picture The Perfect Storm as the remarkably accurate meteorologist who warned of the impending storm. He was played by actor Christopher McDonald.

Todd moved full-time into video marketing in 2006, establishing Squeeze Videos with Derrick Van Dyke, and beginning a new career as a video product promoter. He was also the front man on some of the top products in the Internet marketing arena. His videos began to flood the marketplace, as the products he represented often hit record sales, such as the recent releases of VideoMaker FX and Explaindio Video Creator.

This year Todd has continued to bring new products to the marketplace, such as Green Screen Profit, which brought his love of video making into the hands of his growing fan base. In addition, 2014 marks the year that Todd's affiliate sales have gone through the roof, becoming JVZoo's #1 affiliate and earning over $69,000 in commission in just one day, selling 3,634 units of a moderately low-cost video product.

Todd loves sharing his ability to relate to his email list through special videos that preview and pre-sell upcoming releases in the Internet marketing arena, especially those that have a strong focus on video and video marketing. Other marketers who have modeled his techniques have gone on to be some of the most successful affiliates, dominating leader boards just like Todd does.

Although Todd originally became known as a forecaster of weather, he now has taken a crack at forecasting where video is going in the rest of this decade. He feels that interactive videos for mobile devices will become the wave of the future very soon.

Connect with Todd at:

facebook.com/ToddGrossVideoMarketingExpert

Twitter: @toddgross

Todd Created:

Green Screen Profit shows you how to make "chroma key" videos on your own, the kind where the background disappears and you can place yourself or your subject in front of virtually anything! The equipment needed, the software, and the tricks to do green screen videos on a computer or even an iPad are all

addressed. Todd even shows how to make these green screen videos with no green screen at all!

Learn more at: GreenScreen.Rocks